# A Connected School

## E. Perry Good
## Jeff Grumley
## Shelley Roy

**Illustrations by
Jeffrey Hale**

**NEW VIEW PUBLICATIONS**
Chapel Hill

Illustrated by Jeffrey Hale
Design by Kelly Prelipp Lojk

ISBN: 0-944337-45-7

## This book is dedicated

*... to our families who keep us going and keep the home fires burning:*
**The Goods**: *Fred and Jessica*
**The Grumleys**: *Therese, Bretta, Margaret, Tom, and Ben*
**The Roys**: *Duncan and Wesley*

*... and especially to our mothers, who first taught us to connect!*
**Ethel Highsmith Perry Laffitte, Betty Grumley Bizzy, and Shirley T. Workman.**

## SPECIAL THANKS AND GREAT APPRECIATION TO ...

Jeffrey Hale, our artist, who outdid himself in getting the drawings done with his special creative touch and wit.

Kelly Lojk who edited and designed the book in record time while being cheerful and encouraging.

Fred Good who gave us direction when we needed it and had a lot of input into this book.

Pam Fox who edited and helped with rewriting as we neared the end.

Yvonne Cleveland and Bobbi Whitmore in the New View office who support our workshops in countless ways and get us there with what we need to connect.

# ACKNOWLEDGMENTS

We would like to honor and acknowledge William T. Powers, the originator of Perceptual Control Theory. His body of work over the past thirty years has served as the foundation for our work through the International Association for Applied Control Theory (IAACT).

We would also like to thank William Glasser, who first introduced us to Control Theory. His Reality Therapy questions are the basis of the self-evaluation strategies used in this book.

We would like to express our gratitude to all of the IAACT instructors who have helped in countless ways by sharing their thoughts, ideas, reflections, and experiences with us. They each in their own way daily live the IAACT mission: "Together we build the Art and Heart of Perceptual Control Theory."

We would also like to thank the agencies, schools, and educators who have supported, implemented, and tested the concepts of *A Connected School* with thousands of learners:

* Area Education Agency #267, Cedar Falls, Iowa; especially Ed Redalen, Tricia Elmer, and Sara McInerny
* Cumberland County (North Carolina) Schools, especially Bill Harrison and Carol Hudson

* Step One, Winston-Salem, North Carolina, especially Jane Williams and her staff
* Winston-Salem/Forsyth County (North Carolina) Schools, especially Nancy Dixon
* Binghamton (New York) City School District; especially Peggy Wozniak, Mike Melamed, Mary Cahill, and Patty Gazda Grace
* The Johnson City (New York) Community School District, especially Larry Rowe and Mary Kay Frys
* Marshalltown (Iowa) Community School District, especially Joan Redalen
* Waterloo (Iowa) Community Schools, especially Patrick Clancy
* Eden Prairie (Minnesota) Independent School District, especially Cassandra Schroeder-Erkens and Larry Leebens
* Rockford (Illinois) Public Schools; especially Mike Golden, Vicki Jacobson, and Sue Haney-Bauer
* Midgardtur Family Services, Reykjavik, Iceland, especially Sigbrudur Erla Arnardottir
* Yellowknife School District (Restitution Peace Project) (NWT), especially Lynn Taylor and Arlene Bell
* Greater Clark County (Indiana) Schools, especially Linda Grumley DuFour, Bunny Nash, and Ann Schnepf

# contents

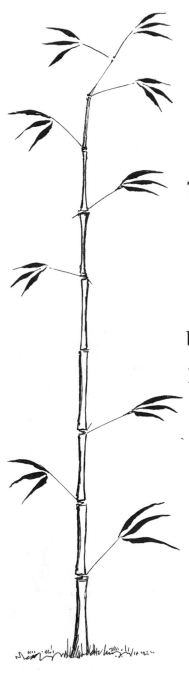

"Perceptual Control Theory is the glue that holds together many strategies that I have used for a long time but did not understand how or why they were supposed to work. Now I do."

*Anita Vanous, teacher*
*Cedar Falls, Iowa*

# foreword

**A** **CONNECTED SCHOOL** is about gaining a better understanding of and connecting to those elements that almost everyone can agree are important for school success. It is not about how to reform the educational system. It is not about a new learning theory. It is not about what is right or wrong with schools. In this book, we unite elements that educators use to succeed into a cohesive, inter-related whole, and tie them to a conceptual framework of how people behave known as Perceptual Control Theory. We attempt in this book to underpin what contemporary educational experts know about school success with a scientific theory of the behavior of all living organisms.

Until now, most school-reform efforts — including the holistic education movement — have been without an adequate understanding of what makes living things different from inanimate things, such as rocks or metal. To a large degree, school reform efforts have relied on what has come to be known as best practices rather than on a science of behavior. Consequently, we have been imposing one program on top of another, with the result that teachers are no longer able to sort them out, much less implement them in their own classrooms.

Perceptual Control Theory teaches us that what distinguish-

**"Every living thing expends energy and will do whatever is needed to preserve itself, including changing."**

*Margaret J. Wheatley*

es the behavior of living things is their ability to create the same results using variable means. This simple understanding leads us to realize that as long as we are teaching people how to deal with the generic "student" in the classroom, we are doing both ourselves and our students a disservice. Each child comes with his or her own goals, not to mention widely varying means for achieving those goals. What will work for one student will not work for the next one. How to manage the education of students given this basic truth is the subject of this book.

We hope to change the culture of schools. Edgar H. Schein, in his book *Organizational Culture and Leadership*, describes the basic assumptions and beliefs shared by members of an organization as the organization's "culture." A school culture based on an understanding of Perceptual Control Theory dramatically affects the way schools make decisions and conduct day-to-day operations. We are convinced that once this new theory is understood and internalized, programs lose their importance and teachers, indeed all of us, are better able to learn and grow based on our own innate talents and abilities.

*A Connected School* is written for classroom teachers who are looking to do two things.

**First** and most important, we want to help you, the teacher, become the educator you want to be and more confident that your instincts about kids and how to work with them are mostly right. You would not be in the teaching profession if you hated being in a classroom full of kids for numerous hours every day, a hundred and eighty days a year. Those instincts that brought you into the profession and that keep you there are important to recognize, understand, and nurture.

**Second**, our goal is to help you better understand what connects you to the kids, how you manage your classroom, and how you can use that knowledge to better help them achieve their own goals.

For all kinds of reasons, we often end up yielding to the idea that students are inanimate objects we must mold and control. We find ourselves

"Do not try to satisfy your vanity by teaching a great many things. Awaken people's curiosity. It is enough to open minds; do not overload them. Put there just a spark. If there is some good inflammable stuff, it will catch fire."

*Anatole France*

working hard to meet other people's objectives rather than our own and those of the kids we teach. We then become enforcers and objects of forces outside ourselves.

Perceptual Control Theory is a scientific theory of human behavior that turns these notions on

their head. Although PCT is a theory and not a law, like the law of gravity, more and more evidence is piling up in its favor. Harvard professor and researcher Alfie Kohn and others have been pointing out for years that we are barking up the wrong tree by trying to control kids from the outside, using rewards and punishments, rather than acting upon the notion that kids too have goals and seek meaning in their own lives. In this book, we show you how to use PCT concepts to become a catalyst to help students discover discipline within themselves, connections to others and to learning, and ultimately to be the people they want to be.

# overview

## A CONNECTED SCHOOL
### is
## ACHIEVING, CARING, and SAFE.

Most schools have one or even two of these characteristics, but few have all these qualities working simultaneously. And even fewer connect these three essential elements into one cohesive approach to education. Nor do schools approach each of these areas from the same theoretical base. Teachers around the globe feel pressured to have their students achieve. Consequently, academic standards and instructional strategies have moved to the forefront of teacher training and education.

However, little effort is made to link student achievement with school climate. Little effort is made to link achievement and school climate to safety. Every new program or approach in each of these areas serves to increase teacher frustration.

## Teachers frequently say, "Don't ask me to add another thing! I don't have time! I can't do it!"

At the heart of the frustration is the lack of connection between all the things educators are asked to do. Even more frustrating is not understanding the connection between what they are asked to do and how the brain operates. Most educators are using an antiquated view of how the brain functions — which includes the idea that it operates from the outside in. A new theory of human motivation and behavior — Perceptual Control Theory — challenges this assumption. In a nutshell, PCT states that **THE BRAIN FUNCTIONS FROM THE INSIDE OUT**. This simple idea connects everything educators are asked to do in the restructuring of education. It challenges the idea that we can control students to get them to do what we want them to do.

In fact, educators know that the only person you can control is yourself. (And sometimes that's even hard to do!) In countless workshops we have asked teachers:

## "Who can you control?"

The answer is always,

## "Only myself."

We then ask them to tell us how much of their day they spend trying to control kids, other staff members, and their own families. The answer frequently is 24-7!

## We know we can't control others, and yet we spend an enormous amount of time and energy trying to do just that.

In *A Connected School* the aim is to have connected people controlling themselves — whether these people are teachers, counselors, students, principals, assistants, custodians, or bus drivers.

**W**illiam Powers, the originator of Perceptual Control Theory, says, "People controlling people, that's the problem. And it's mainly caused by ignorance not ill will ... by not understanding the difference between an inanimate object and a living system." In most schools around the country an average of about five hundred living control systems arrive each morning. In some high schools, two thousand living control systems arrive. Is it any wonder we have problems!

Especially when some of the living control systems — teachers — think that they have to control the other living control systems — students. In order to control students, teachers use rewards, punishments, guilt, and praise. In the short run, these controlling behaviors usually work. In the long run, the result is kids who rebel — either now or later — and kids who withdraw — either now or later. (Kids tattoo themselves, drink, use drugs, or surf the 'net 24-7.) In other words, these kids do not have discipline within.

One of the prime ways to develop discipline within is to master the theory of internal control and purposeful behavior. When we understand the theory and operate based on it, we help ourselves and those we work with. We can use Perceptual Control Theory to connect and communicate more effectively and efficiently.

Our goal is to help educators see that it is worth taking the time to learn a complex theory because it will connect with and enhance what is already occurring in the areas of achievement, caring, and safety. If we can create a dynamic balance between these three components, we can create greater capacity exponentially in each area.

*A Connected School* is not about school in the traditional sense. It is about the people in the school. And this book's primary focus is not on the kids in the school. Instead we focus on the adults. Because if we don't change how we think about behavior and what we are doing, it is unlikely that the kids will change. It's like an algebraic equation. If one element changes the whole equation is altered.

> "If there is anything that we wish to change in the child, we should first examine it and see whether it is not something that could better be changed in ourselves."
>
> *Carl Jung*

In school reform we have been looking for ways to change students or change the system without understanding that we ourselves have to change in a fundamental way. The place to start is *not* by introducing another "approach" to discipline or instructional strategies or school climate or whatever the current "issue" happens to be. The place to start is a personal change — the hardest change there is and perhaps the only meaningful one. We invite you to fundamentally change the way you think about people, behavior, safety, and learning.

There is certainly no shortage of research telling us what we should be doing in our schools. In fact, we are amazed at the amount of research out there that educators are asked to keep up with. Recently, researchers at the University of Minnesota took a hard look at data collected by the Add Health Study — the largest study ever done on adolescents.✖

The report states: "In an earlier study, researchers at the University of Minnesota learned that school connectedness is a powerful protective factor. Their research showed that students who feel connected to school:

✱ are less likely to use alcohol and illegal drugs;

✱ are less likely to engage in violent or deviant behaviors;

✱ are less likely to become pregnant; and

✱ are less likely to experience emotional distress."

At the heart of *A Connected School* are educators who have truly made the shift from an external focus to an internal one. They understand the scientific theory of internal motivation and purpose-

✖ *Improving the Odds: The Untapped Power of Schools to Improve the Health of Teens* (2002), authored by R.W. Blum, C.A. McNeely, and P.M. Rinehart of the Center for Adolescent Health and Development, University of Minnesota. The report was based on analysis of data from the University of North Carolina's Add Health Study.

ful behavior. They understand that this theory explains why some of the latest instructional strategies (such as Constructivist Learning and Quantum Learning strategies) successfully promote achievement — because they are strategies that operate from the inside out. They understand that a positive school climate is created when everyone in the school learns to control himself or herself.

These educators are engaged in the process of personal change. This takes years, not days or weeks. It also takes a commitment from the top leadership. As we all know, change is difficult. But change is not impossible. Many schools have made a commitment to the idea of internal rather than external control. In this book, you will hear from educators who have made a commitment to this kind of change and how it is working for them.

This book provides an overview of Perceptual Control Theory and shows you how the theory relates to caring, safety, and achievement. We will give you some simple ideas based on PCT that you can use to move toward dynamic balance for yourself, your classroom, your school, or your educational system.

We have organized this book and its three major chapters so that they reflect what we consider to be a logical order of priorities if we are to remain consistent with Perceptual Control Theory. The most important agents in affecting school improvement are classroom teachers. We think that it is important always to begin any process of evaluation with our-selves. By looking at our own thinking and behavior, we are upholding one of the main messages of PCT, that we can only control ourselves.

Through reflection and self-evaluation, teachers can have a profound effect on how schools operate. By looking thoughtfully and honestly at our own expe-riences and the role we play in them, we can begin to learn the process of self-regulation. And thus we become better able to model the behaviors we want from our students. In each of the main chapters we ask you to reflect on your beliefs. This is followed by identifying some of the issues facing schools and a description of how *A Connected School* might better address these issues based on an understanding of PCT. Each section concludes with you, the teacher, reflecting on how you relate the chapter's content to your daily practices.

# Perceptual Control Theory

**W**hen someone on an airplane or at a party asks me what I do for a living, I say, "I teach and help others understand Hierarchical Perceptual Control Theory or PCT for short." The universal response to this is a furrowed brow and "What's that?" I proceed to tell them that it is a scientific theory of human behavior. By this time most people have usually decided that they are no longer interested in what I do. Why? Not because they aren't interested in human behavior, but because they heard the word "scientific." This often brings back nightmares of complex equations, experiments that never came out the way

11

*the textbooks said they were supposed to, and vocabulary rarely used outside of high school. So why do I continue to use the word "scientific" when I tell people what I do? Because "scientific" implies a great deal more than my own personal thinking about a subject or idea.*

— SHELLEY ROY

Science has been described as the never-ending search for answers to the universe's mysteries. The process of science is intended to help us understand the "truths" or general laws of our world. Based on these truths we then make decisions about when and how to apply them, as well as weigh the potential benefits of our chosen applications against potential risks. This is in essence what we are asking you to do — examine your present practices as they relate to PCT.

Science by its nature is both an area of study and a process. Scientific understanding was once thought to be information about an objective world out there (Descartes), but this is no longer true. We have learned we cannot separate the knower from what is known. The beliefs, values, and experiences of the scientist directly impact the results and actions of science. According to Fritjof Capra, "Scientific facts emerge out of an entire constellation of human perceptions, values, and action — in a word, out of a paradigm — from which they cannot be separated." You can only operate based on your own personal frame of reference. Unlike Descartes, today's scientists understand that the universe is not "out there" but includes us as well as everything else. Let's begin the scientific journey by having you reflect on your personal paradigm of science and human behavior.

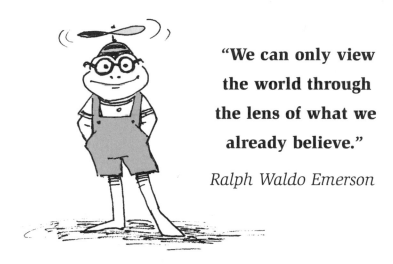

"We can only view the world through the lens of what we already believe."

*Ralph Waldo Emerson*

So take a moment, close your eyes, and reflect. What do you believe about science? What do you believe about human behavior?

As a subject, science is intended to help us unravel our world and gain understanding of it. As a process, science is a procedure for systematically pursuing knowledge. These pursuits of understanding involve intellectual inventiveness, the creation of mental images of what has never been actually experienced, and the devising and testing of strong intuitive feelings. It's believing without seeing.

A scientist then is someone who through a systematic approach pursues understanding natural phenomena, proposes a theory about the phenomena, and then spends the rest of his life trying to prove himself wrong. William Powers, the originator of Perceptual Control Theory is such a scientist. In particular, Powers is a scientist who uses

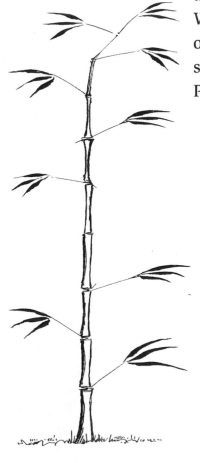

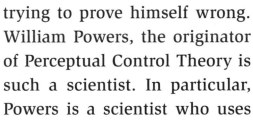

**"Thinking like a scientist does not require incredibly precise, highly sophisticated, otherworldly logic. ... Science is nothing but trained and organized common sense."**

*Charles Wynn &*
*Arthur Wiggins*

model building to test his theory. A model is a representation or likeness of reality invented to account for observed phenomena. Model airplanes, model railroads, model boats, and computer simulations (the most common method used to test PCT) are all examples of something real, but in a different size, material, or complexity than the thing it is modeled after.

Perceptual Control Theory is based on the scientific understanding that **all living systems operate to seek dynamic balance**. It is a simple theory in that it is based upon a few core principles, but also a complex one in that it involves intricate interconnections created by the system as a whole. William Powers and his colleagues believe PCT can accurately explain more than 99 percent of human behavior.

Theories are our best attempts, at any given moment in time, to explain the world around us. All of us operate out of theory. We call it gut feelings, common sense, beliefs, or values. Many teachers are *unconsciously* skilled. They are either a naturally skilled teacher or they experiment through trial and error until they become skilled. The problem is that they are effective teachers without knowing why. When we understand theory it provides two things: an ability to be *consciously* skilled and the freedom to explore how to truly engage our students.

> **"Without understanding of theory, implementation is often tainted."**

## So how do you explain Perceptual Control Theory at a party?

PCT may be thought of as **the plant view of life**. Plants are living systems that grow, change, need nourishment, thrive in healthy environments, and always grow better, stronger, and faster with a bit of tender loving care. By taking a close look at nature, we can gain great insight into human behavior and human systems. The plant view of human behavior has at its core four fundamental concepts.

**First,** living systems are constantly seeking dynamic balance.

**Second,** living systems operate from the inside out. (It is the system's internal references compared against perceptions of the outside world that let the system know if it is or is not in a state of dynamic balance.)

**Third,** living systems are continuously engaged in the circular process of feedback.

**Fourth,** living systems operate at multiple levels, with the higher levels sending reference messages to lower levels.

Unfortunately most of us have lived our lives based on a different theory, which might be thought of as **the rock view of human motivation**. The rock view is cemented in physical laws that were intended to describe non-living objects or systems. Such physical laws help answer questions like: "What do we need to do to create a machine that can fly?" or "How do I build a building that is fifty stories high?" One of the best understood tenets of this worldview goes something like this: For every action there is an opposite and equal reaction. When we operate on the rock view of human motivation, we believe that we have the ability to get anybody to do what we want, if we can just take the right "action." We only need to know how to use a lever, a pulley, or some other simple machine to get what we want. Most of us are familiar with this view and have heard others say, "He made me do it." ... "If she wouldn't have [fill in the blank] I wouldn't have [fill in the blank]." ... "If you do this, you'll get that." ... or "If you don't do this, here's what will happen."

This view leads to learning literally millions of strategies and techniques, because the premise of the rock view is that with the right words, ges-

tures, or actions I can get anyone to do just about anything. In moving the rock, no matter how large, if I use enough leverage or wear the rock down into small pieces I can be fairly assured that I can move the rock where I want. Similarly with people, if I use enough leverage (reward, threaten, praise) or wear them down (by needling, nagging, preaching, or applying pressure) I can be fairly assured that I can get them to do what I want.

What is most amazing about this theory is that even though we have both historical and personal experiences that have proven it wrong time and again, we still cling to *the rock view*. Why? Because it tells us that we can control others. As a parent, teacher, preacher, administrator, or boss we can control our kids, students, parishioners, staff, and employees. A corollary belief to the idea of controlling others is that it is unrealistic to expect children to do what they are "supposed to do" in the absence of incentives, be they intangible (such as praise or good grades) or tangible (such as money or presents).

Imagine how freeing it would be to stop spending all of your time trying to control other people. The truth is you cannot control someone else! In fact, most of us have a hard enough time controlling ourselves. Furthermore, wouldn't it be nice if we could figure out how to do a better job with ourselves, improving our teaching skills and our ability to lead?

**But, like most things in life, what is freeing is also frightening.** In some ways, it is frightening to acknowledge that I cannot control others. If that is true, what power do I have as a parent, teacher, preacher, administrator, or boss? Luckily, nature is designed to balance freedom and fright. It is the seeking of dynamic balance that sustains nature, and understanding Perceptual Control Theory can help you keep in balance.

The kind of balance we are talking about is dynamic (much like the concept of Yin and Yang) not static. We often trap ourselves into *the rock view* by thinking of balance as a teeter-totter. In grade school we use to play a game, which in the

Midwest was called "farmer-farmer." One of us had her feet on the ground and the other was high up in the air. The one up in the air would say, "Farmer, farmer, let me down." The one with her feet firmly planted on the ground would ask, "What will you give me?" When the person in the air finally figured out something that the one on the ground wanted, the roles were reversed. The game was either/or — either you were up in the air or you were down on the ground. How often do we get caught thinking of balance as either/or: either I get what I want or the other person does?

How often do we pause to think about whether what we are asking children to do is really necessary? Are we thinking about how to help the child become a responsible, self-regulating person, or do we just want to get the child to obey? Often when we get trapped into either/or thinking — seeing the world as pairs of polar opposites — we lose sight of the rules of nature and thus lose dynamic balance. For example, either you are controlling or you are permissive, either you crack down hard or you let kids get away with anything. Looking at the world in this way is like looking at a black-and-white photo and seeing it simply as that — black and white. This perspective isn't necessarily wrong, it just doesn't reveal the beauty, clarity, and quality of the photo. Similarly, the nuances of shadow and light, contrast, and the infinite shades of grey help us see the complexity of the world — a world where there is magnificence, dimension, and distinction created by nature's dance of dynamic balance. Andrea Christopher, a counselor in Cedar Falls, Iowa, put it this way: "It is like giving me a new pair of glasses, or showing me colors in a painting that I had never seen before. ... Learning the theory, practicing the questioning techniques, doing a tremendous amount of self-evaluation, and getting feedback has made the difference in me at my very core."

When psychology first came into vogue, the most popular line of thought was that of *the rock view* of human behavior. Early psychology was based mostly on experiments with rats, pigeons, and a few dogs. The premise was that the semi-starved rat in the box, with virtually nothing to do but press on a lever for food, would provide an accurate explanation of human behavior. The beliefs drawn from these experiments were that animals, including humans, could be externally controlled and taught to do just about anything. That takes us back to the premise that for every action there is an opposite and equal reaction. Something outside of us can control us.

It took the atrocities in concentration camps during World War II and other events of the time to force many theorists to question the premise that humans could be externally controlled. A classic example of this shift in thinking is documented in the works of Victor Frankl. In *Man's Search for Meaning*, Frankl describes his personal experience of attempts to dehumanize man at the concentration camps of Auschwitz and Dachau. To Frankl's amazement, hundreds of people refused to give up, give in, or commit suicide while under the constant threat of torture and death. Frankl's experience led him to what has been termed "the humanization of psychiatry." Thus came the shift in focus from external events to internal references as an explanation for why people do what they do.

This was a giant step in the right direction. It changed the focus from control outside of the system to inside of the system. For example, teachers often say: "All my students want is attention, and they don't care if they get it in a positive or a negative way." At the core of this sentiment is the idea that one action causes an equal and opposite reaction. The belief that there is a direct link from what a person is doing to what they want is linear, not circular.

---

**In Perceptual Control Theory**, understanding behavior is premised on the idea that **"behavior is the control of perception."** Behavior is neither a reaction to an external stimulus nor a reaction to internal stimulus. It is our natural attempt to stay in dynamic balance. **Our world is a combination of the interplay between our perception and our environment.**

et us use a metaphor from which we can build a basic understanding of PCT. Think for a minute about cooking. Imagine that you are trapped in a snowstorm, can't get to the grocery store or the local golden arches, and you have to make dinner with what's in the fridge and cupboards. How would you begin? Imagine what you would do throughout the process and what the end product would look, smell, and taste like. First imagine yourself with familiar ingredients, and then imagine yourself with an odd combination of ingredients. If you don't perceive yourself as a cook, think about something else ... like walking into someone else's classroom without a lesson plan.

So where do you start? Who knows? That's part of the point here. **One key idea in understanding PCT is that there really is no beginning and no end.** There are no direct-link actions, as there are in a stimulus-response world. In the classroom, our personal references of a student steer our behavior, and our behavior impacts our perception. It is a cycle that neither the student nor we can escape. This idea, that in PCT we call "circular causality," is very familiar to any one who has never quite perfected a recipe or taught the perfect lesson.

If you are a semi-accomplished cook, you  know it is difficult to create the exact same dish twice. For instance, perhaps one day the carrots are sweeter, or maybe the tomatoes are more acidic, or maybe you simply combined the ingredients in a different order. And if you teach, you know how difficult it is to teach the exact same lesson twice. In fact, it is impossible. Maybe there is a full moon out, and it's the day before spring break. Perhaps you got interrupted with a fire drill in the middle of class. The point is that not only are there no direct links in actions, there are no two environmental settings that present the exact same conditions. You can't step into the same river twice.

**Remember two core principles:** Perceptual Control Theory is based on circular causality (not linear cause and effect), and we never do exactly the same action twice. Why? Because the environmental context is never exactly the same. Small shifts in the environment may call for different actions to produce the same results. **It is being able to produce nearly the same results by variable means that makes life exciting.** We are faced daily with new learning experiences. And isn't it grand that we can be so flexible under all the changing conditions!

Let's get back to our cooking and take a closer look at circular causality. If you are a great cook (or have been around someone who is) you understand this concept delectably. In cooking, it is the sampling spoon. It is the process of letting the dish set for a time and then tasting it and adding a bit and tasting it and adding a bit and tasting it and still thinking as you sit down to eat, it needs a bit more pepper. In the classroom it is talking to the students and seeing that half of them don't understand and then giving another example. Then ten minutes after class is over, we may think of a different example that we believe would have cleared up all of the confusion. We have our reference for how the dish should taste, how the lesson should go, and we keep adjusting our behavior until the dish or the lesson is as close to our reference as we can get it.

Take the example of the Goldilocks fairy tale. She kept trying out beds until she found one that came close to matching her reference for a bed that was "just right." Papa Bear's bed, too hard; Mama Bear's bed, too soft; and Baby Bear's bed,

"It is no simple matter to pause in the midst of one's maturity, when life is full of function, to examine what are the principles that control that functioning."

*Pearl S. Buck*

just right. Goldilocks and Baby Bear shared a similar reference for how a bed should feel. We constantly check to see if what we are "taking in" matches our reference, looking for a balance between what we think we are "taking in" and what we want it to be. We only add more spices (behave) when there isn't a match between our perception (how we have taken in the world) and our reference (how we think it should be).

The last key idea we want you to understand about PCT is that these circular loops operate on multiple levels, with the higher levels sending reference messages to lower levels. The picture I carry in my mind's eye is that of a giant spider web that when examined from space is one massive web but when examined under a microscope is composed of millions of smaller webs.✖

Fritjof Capra put it this way: "Life consists of networks within networks. At each scale, under closer scrutiny, the nodes of the network reveal themselves as smaller networks. We tend to arrange these systems, all nesting within larger systems, in a hierarchical scheme by placing the larger systems above the smaller one in a pyramid fashion. But this is

✖ There are two great children's books that illustrate this concept quite nicely. They are *ZOOM* and *REZOOM*, both by Istvan Banyai, available through Puffin Books (1995).

human projection. In nature there is no 'above' or 'below' and there are no hierarchies. There are only networks nesting within other networks."

I n terms of PCT, William Powers proposes that there are eleven levels ranging from "intensity" to "systems concepts." No, we don't want you to memorize them. What's important for you to know is that the levels exist.

## You should also understand that we can only operate from the level we presently perceive and down.

Therefore, when working with others, we want to operate at the highest level possible.

The six lower levels involve the way we take in the world and include sensory information. They are concrete, quickly processed, and specific. The next couple of levels are how we label or name incoming information (such as knowing the names of colors or being able to identify a cup as a cup, regardless of its size and shape). The next levels, the program and sequence levels are generally thought of as the "doing" levels. Examples of these levels include giving a test, ringing a bell, or following rules. The two highest levels include principles and a system of values (what Powers calls "systems concepts"). The first includes our values and beliefs, the second is our own core understanding of how the world operates and includes our references for who we want to be in the world. These highest levels are abstract, slowly processed, and general. What we want to do in schools is "bump it up." We want to operate not from the perspective of what to do, but from the perspective of who we want to be in the world.

In a nutshell, PCT states that living systems are constantly attempting to create dynamic balance. This includes the ability of a system to coexist with other systems. It is our attempt to keep in dynamic balance that explains why we always see what we don't want or what's wrong.

**We are naturally designed to look for where the system is out of balance and try to lessen the imbalance.**

Our actions are based on which imbalance our awareness is focused at any given moment. For example, if you have been reading for a long period of time, you may be sensing an imbalance in the comfort of your posterior. Or perhaps you have become focused on the imbalance of the moisture content of your mouth. (You are thirsty.) Now that your awareness is drawn to those imbalances you may seek to lessen the error by moving, getting up, and getting a drink. Or maybe you see that you're near the end of the chapter and decide to "bump it up" to keep your awareness focused on the imbalance of wanting to finish and being finished.

What does all this mean for our work in schools? It means that instead of attempting to externally control others, self-regulation comes naturally. We are like plants growing towards the sun, naturally seeking what we need to stay alive. It means we want kids to be in charge of themselves — kids doing the right thing when no one's looking. Ideally, it means a world where kids and adults keep themselves in dynamic balance while coexisting with each other.

So how do we know which theory we are acting upon — the rock view or the plant view of human behavior? Listen to yourself and those

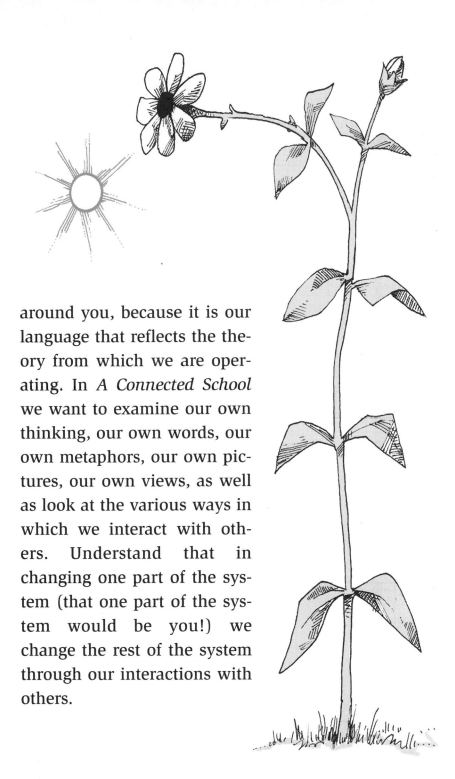

around you, because it is our language that reflects the theory from which we are operating. In *A Connected School* we want to examine our own thinking, our own words, our own metaphors, our own pictures, our own views, as well as look at the various ways in which we interact with others. Understand that in changing one part of the system (that one part of the system would be you!) we change the rest of the system through our interactions with others.

# Assumptions

**GET THE PICTURE**

**I** teach beginning band students in the fifth grade. To help calm the chaos that occurs during every band rehearsal, I decided to give each student a particular "job" to do for the setup and takedown of the rehearsal center. All the jobs seemed to be self-explanatory to me — move the tables back, put the stands away, store the percussion equipment, put the chairs in order, etc. I wanted to make sure every student had a very specific, significant job so no one felt left out of the process.

I had enough jobs for everyone and very carefully began to pair each student with a corresponding responsibility. I was really looking forward to seeing how well my new idea would work. After our first attempt to complete the jobs, I found nearly as much — or in some cases even more — chaos than before.

What I thought was a self-explanatory job (because I had a solid reference point) was unfamiliar territory to my students.

The following week during small group les-

sons, I took the time to demonstrate and teach the expected way for each student to execute the job that was assigned to him or her.

In the process of doing this, I could see the relief on the faces of my students. Earlier, they were reluctant to ask "silly" question such as, "How do I put a stand away?" But the real problem was my own — in not realizing that the students lacked a reference point.

Little did I realize I had to teach a student to push the stand all the way down, flatten the top part, face them all in the same direction, and only stack one stand on top of another in order for them to fit into the allotted space.

Once each student had the opportunity to learn how to do his or her job, the tasks were accomplished easily, quickly, quietly, AND correctly. Not only did it accomplish getting the room put back the way it was before, but each student also assumed an element of pride and self-respect for being a part of the entire process.

What a major difference that lesson made in the way I approach my teaching.

KATHY McCORMACK
WATERLOO (IOWA)
COMMUNITY SCHOOLS

# Live It!

**I** have been struggling with following a diet and exercise routine. My most recent effort has lasted for almost three months, and I have had some great successes. I am running longer and faster, and I have shed a bunch of pounds. Compliments on how I look have come from many different people. Still, I have found myself being inconsistent. I am a month behind where I could have been if I did not fluctuate. I took some time today to write out my thoughts.

My first question: What kind of person do I want to be? My answer: I want to be a healthy and physically fit person. So what principles should I live by to be who I want to be? I will exercise five days per week. I will follow a proper diet. I will seek out ways to relax.

After I typed the above, I thought, "Yeah. So. It's not like I don't know this stuff." This is what I want, yet I am so inconsistent. So I looked at my answer again. *I really thought about it.* I realized that my answer was just about me. After all, doesn't the kind of person I want to be impact my family? When we are talking about values, does-

n't the concept of systems come into play? So I changed my answer: "I want to live and model a healthy and physically fit lifestyle."

When I was done typing and looked at that sentence, I could not believe how different it was for me. I realized that my being healthy and physically fit meant less to me as an individual than when compared to my responsibility and desire as a parent to model the same for my children. You have to love this PCT "stuff"!

**TOM LALLY**
PRINCIPAL, JOHNSON CITY
(NEW YORK) COMMUNITY
SCHOOL DISTRICT

# caring

## MAKE THAT CONNECTION!

found myself in a classroom on the Lower East Side of Manhattan, armed with a master's degree in education from New York University. That surely meant that I knew what I was doing, right? It was January 3 and I was desperate for a job. I heard they needed teachers at P.S. 71, a junior high

*school on Avenue B between Sixth and Seventh Streets. I signed my contract and then found out that I was the eleventh teacher these kids had had since September. When it dawned on me that ten people had already tried this job and failed, I became a little nervous. When I found out the teacher before me had never even quit, she had just been seen running down Sixth Street scream-ing, I became truly worried. Would I be able to handle these kids when ten other people could not? As classes started, I began to wonder. Nothing that I had been taught at New York University had any-thing to do with the reality in my classrooms. (I moved to a different classroom each period of the day — no place to call home.) My professors had-n't prepared me for scenarios like P.S. 71.*

*In spite of the fact that the school had some dan-gerous qualities, I liked the kids. They were, under-neath it all, just regular eighth-graders — sassy, adorable, out of control, and caring. They acted like four-years-old one minute, and twenty-two-year-olds the next. As I began to know them better, I asked them about teacher #10. The students said they had emptied the contents of her purse into a metal trash can in the classroom, set it on fire, and then thrown in the purse. She left screaming. I asked them why they did it. They looked around the classroom at each other, and I could tell they were wondering whether or not to share this information with me. Finally, one of the girls, Elsie, quietly said, "She wouldn't touch us." Those words still echo in my head after all these years. What these kids wanted, like all kids want, was to simply have their teacher treat them like human beings, to touch them, to care about them, to connect with them.*

– PERRY GOOD

**W**hy do we need a chapter in this book connecting caring to achievement and safety? Because caring isn't in most educators' job descriptions — achievement and safety are. Caring is the unwritten part of your job. But caring is the crucial element that helps to produce a school climate that is positive and supportive of both achievement and safety. Maybe this fact seems self-evident to you, but some teachers say, "Caring is not part of my job; my job is to teach." The aim of this chapter is to help you see that connecting with your students, promoting a positive climate in your classroom, and creating the level of safety you want for your students is the background tapestry for helping your students — and you! — achieve what you want.

**What exactly is school climate?** Here is a definition from R.H. Moos: *School climate is the social atmosphere of a learning environment.* Moos divides social environments into three categories.

**1** Relationship, which includes involvement, affiliation with others in the classroom, and teacher support.

**2** Personal growth or goal orientation, which includes the personal development and self-enhancement of all members of the environment.

**3** System maintenance and system change, which includes the orderliness of the environment.

In this part of the book we will look at relationship and personal growth. The chapter on safety discusses system maintenance and change and its connection to discipline within. If you look at these three categories, people in schools seem to spend a lot of time on system maintenance and system change and not much on relationship and personal growth.

Does this ring true for you? Sometimes when teachers do spend time on relationships and personal growth, they are hesitant to let others know, lest they be accused of not taking achievement seriously.

**P**erceptual Control Theory emerged out of the scientific exploration of quantum physics and living systems, thus providing a better understanding of human behavior. In the quantum world, everything is seen as interconnected by a vast network. Fritjof Capra, author of *The Web of Life*, describes life, even at the subatomic level, as "a set of relationships that reach outward to other things." Therefore, at the heart of *A Connected School* are the relationships in that school. If the relationships work, the school works. All the peo-

> "None of us exists independent of our relationships with others. Different settings and people evoke some qualities from us and leave others dormant. In each of these relationships we are different, new in some way."
>
> *Margaret Wheatley*

ple in the school are connected: teacher to teacher, student to student, teacher to student, teacher to administrator, teacher to parent. School becomes a place where people *want* to be instead of *have* to be. For example, Superintendent Bill Harrison says the goal of Cumberland County Schools in North Carolina is to have "students who *want* to come to school."

A quantum theorist describes particles not as separate entities but as interrelated energy patterns in an ongoing dynamic process. That pretty much describes any group of students in a classroom, doesn't it? Reality for a living system is all about relationships. Who do you have a good relationship with that you never talk to? The answer, of course, is "Nobody." (Though once a teacher in one of our workshops replied, "My husband!") If we carry this idea of good relationships to its logical conclusion, it also means that part of the reason kids don't get along (and why we have so many discipline problems) is that they don't know each other. Bullying, taunting, and all the issues about students getting along with each other seem to be greatly minimized when students know each other well. **We are much more alike on the inside than we are different on the outside.** But, in order to have meaningful relationships you have to develop them. You have to spend time getting to know your students and helping them to know each other. This is not magic. It's not that some people can do it and others can't. It's simply a matter of taking the time to DO IT! (It does help if you know what to do, and we'll talk about that later in the chapter.)

What happens when students don't feel like the teacher cares? They usually do either one of two things, they act out or they withdraw. Remember the kids in P.S. 71 who set the teacher's pocket book ablaze. The students obviously felt that that teacher didn't care about them. Educators are at their wit's end with discipline problems. Students are routinely banished from the classroom and sent to the principal or assistant principal. Sometimes these kids get suspended. Educators are also troubled by students who do nothing or very little in class. But when these students feel connected to the teacher, their motivation to work increases.

Connections help students trust in themselves, each other, and you, the teacher. Deep connections help ease the fears that many of us live with daily. In *Connect*, Harvard Medical School psychiatrist Edward Hallowell says,

*"What is connection, or what I sometimes call connectedness? It is a feeling of being a part of something larger than yourself. The something may be a friendship, a marriage, a team, a school, a company, an activity you love, a country, even a set of ideals, like the Bill of Rights or a belief system, like religion. That feeling of connectedness leads to health and achievement."*

In a study Hallowell conducted at Exeter he found that 80 percent of the students he studied felt connected. He says, "In every measure of mental health and happiness that we used, as well as every measure of achievement, the students who did the best were the connected students."

**The evidence is in!** School climate and achievement are connected. Professor Herbert Walberg at the University of Illinois at Chicago has found that "classroom social environ-

---

**The brain is a social brain and changes in response to engagement with others. Part of our identity depends on establishing community and finding ways to belong. Learning is profoundly influenced by social relationships.**

*Renate Nummela Caine & Geoffrey Caine*

ment is one of the chief psychological determinants of academic learning." Research by R.H. Moos in 1991 determined that "in optimal environments, children, adolescents, and adults enjoy themselves more and get more done." In a report entitled *Improving the Odds: The Untapped Power of Schools to Improve the Health of Teens*, researchers found that "when middle and high school students feel cared for by people at their school and when they feel like they are part of school, they are less likely to engage in unhealthy behaviors. When they feel connected to school they also report higher levels of emotional well being." When students are engaged in healthy behaviors and are emotionally healthy, it stands to reason that they can achieve more.

So why is it that many of our students don't feel connected to school? Most educators do care. You care — if you didn't you wouldn't be working in a school. The pay is relatively low, and long hours are required to do everything from prepare complicated lesson plans to bus duty. You have to care! Yet most students think their teachers don't care about them; they think teachers are against them. In fact, in many of our schools the atmosphere is like a war zone. It's an us-against-them mentality. Why does this condition exist in so many schools? If you wanted to be engaged in combat, you could have joined the military!

Students also care. Sometimes it doesn't seem like they care, but deep down inside, they do. They want to have friends, they want to achieve, they want to be a part of something bigger than themselves — to feel connected. In *The Heart of Learning: Spirituality in Education*, Steven Glazer says, "The struggle comes down to a split about how to deal with (or heal) a very human, very personal sense of disconnection: one that threatens to tear apart not merely individuals, schools, and communities but the living fabric of our world as well. … The heart of learning is revealed within each one of us: rooted in the spirit. By moving inside to the core of our experience, and working out from there … the real work of integration and healing can begin."

In *The Brighter Side of Human Nature*, Alfie Kohn says, "There is good evidence to support the

proposition that it is as 'natural to help as it is to hurt.' In short, the cynical consensus about our species is out of step with the hard data." If you honestly believe your students care, the way you go about managing your classroom is different. Over the past decade, the character education movement has taken hold. That's after a previous decade of bashing talk of values in the classroom. In reality, we are constantly communicating values to students in school, whether we recognize it or not.

Perceptual Control Theory informs us that the brain takes in the world from the lower levels of perception (sensory) and moves to the higher levels (principles, beliefs, and a system of values).

When you manage your classroom secure in this knowledge, you can explore with your students what is important to them and you at the higher levels of perception. How do they want to be treated? How do they want to treat others? But before this work can begin, kids have to feel connected. It starts internally; it doesn't come from the outside. Think of the "character" words posted on many classroom walls — honesty, responsibility, etc. The question is not whether the kids know what the words mean; most of them do. The question is how to make these words operational in the daily activities of school, and to connect these words to the goal of *A Connected School*: creating a dynamic balance of achievement, caring, and safety.

You went into education to work with kids. A central question to ask yourself is: "What kind of educator do I want to be?" Successful, happy, strong, responsible, in control, and caring? And yet, time after time in school we find ourselves not living up to the idea of who we want to be. We find ourselves not living up to the ideals that brought us into education in the first place. A school administrator once said, "People go into education because they love kids and want to help them. After a month in the classroom they hate kids and want to kill them!"

## How do you return to the ideals that brought you into education and become the kind of educator you want to be?

You can start by learning what Perceptual Control Theory teaches about how you perceive yourself.

If you operate from the higher levels (*what you believe* and *who you want to BE in the world*), you connect the mid levels (*what you want to DO in the world*) and lower levels (*how you take in the world*) to your ideals.

Most of the time in school you are focused on what you are doing. You are not focused on who you are being or on the kind of educator you want to be. You are not focusing your students on what they believe and who they want to be. Instead, you are focused on the lower levels of perception — labeling and programs — having students score better on achievement tests and labeling them when they don't!

So, when you are being held accountable for higher test scores, are you disregarding the research on school climate and connecting with students? The research clearly proves there is a relationship between achievement and caring.

Chances are that it is not a matter of your disregarding the research, but rather a matter of not knowing how to incorporate the research findings into your classroom. Do you know HOW to connect with your students? Do you know HOW to establish a positive climate in your classroom without losing control of the class? Do you know how to be the kind of educator you want to be?

> **"While we may take something like simple courtesy for granted — as we did clean air before there was pollution — we may find that it is in fact a precious social achievement that has been hard won over ages of human life and culture, and that once lost or squandered it will be extremely costly to recover."**
>
> *Kenneth Lux*

Do you know how to do this without being considered a "hippie," a bleeding heart, a weirdo, or worse? The excuse heard most often is this one: "I don't have time." But if you are serious about improving academic achievement, then you have to be serious about taking the time to create a positive classroom climate.

When you think about caring, try not to think of it as some sort of Pollyanna approach to your students. We have known some pretty gruff teachers whose students knew they cared. We've also known some saccharin sweet ones whose students knew it was all a show. If you are uncomfortable with the term "caring" think of it as connecting in some way with each of your students.

## How do we connect?

* From the inside out.
* On many levels, from the superficial to the profound.
* Moment by moment.

There is another, more subtle reason that teachers are sometimes hesitant to develop relationships with students: fear of losing control. Perceptual Control Theory teaches us an entirely different perspective of control. Control is what we do to keep ourselves in balance. Your relationship with your students is a large factor in the amount of control you actually have. For many years we have consulted with group homes, detention centers, youth prisons, and wilderness programs for troubled teenagers. One of the main principles we teach is that the only kind of control you have over these kids comes from your connection with them. Time and time again we have found this to be true.

Remember that the only person you can control is yourself. When you try to control students you essentially destroy your relationship with them. Since building a relationship leads to connectedness, and connectedness leads to achievement, then it is important to be aware of how relationships can be undermined. What you can do is help students learn to control themselves.✖ Giving up the belief that you can control others is difficult, but not impossible. Thousands of educators have done it, and so can YOU. A simple way to do this is to frequently ask yourself two questions:

## "Who can I control?"

## "Who do I want to be?"

You can slowly but surely learn to let go of the notion that you can control others, and you can slowly but surely move toward being the kind of educator you want to be.

✖ See *Helping Kids Help Themselves*, by E. Perry Good. New View Publications (1992).

**CONNECTION.** Connection is a function of time and meaning. In order to make strong connections you have to put in a fair amount of time with another person and you have to talk to him about something that is meaningful to both of you. It can go either way. In fact, if you are going to connect, it has to go both ways!

**TIME.** It takes time to connect with others. If you use a little bit of time each day to connect with your students, you will see a difference in how they treat themselves, each other, and you. It doesn't have to be for an entire class period each day. **A little connecting goes a long way.** You connect moment by moment with your students. Tiny connections grow into big ones. A touch, a handshake, a quick comment like, "I heard you were sick, I hope you are feeling better." Simply calling your students by their names helps you to connect. Such small, seemingly insignificant acts can go a long way toward strengthening your relationship to your students.

**MEANING.** Rachael Remen, a medical educator says, "In the medical culture, we do not engage with our full humanity. In fact, authentic human connection — connecting to the humanness in yourself and others — is actually seen as being something undesirable, unprofessional, even dangerous." The same could also be said sometimes for educators. The same bias exists. We fear authentic human connection and yet this is what we (you, me, our students) most want.

# MAKE THAT CONNECTION
**There are two kinds of connections we make with our students:**

## informal
## &
## formal

We connect in **informal** ways daily. "I see you got a new haircut, Shannon. Do you like it?" One teacher shared this with her class of high school juniors: "We found out last night that IBM is cutting more jobs, and this might affect my husband's position. I'm worried about it today, so I may seem a bit preoccupied. But I still want to do a good job as your teacher. So let me know if I don't seem like I'm paying attention. Do any of you have a family member affected by job cuts? Do you think worrying can affect the work you do in school?" Boosting the amount of time you spend sharing things with your students can do wonders for improving kids' sense of connectedness.

The other kinds of connections are built by using **formal** or structured involvement activities. It is essential in *A Connected School* to do lots of connecting activities during the first week of school. These connections will form the link between achievement and safety. If you are a high school teacher, this is a big job. If you have

your students wear name tags (you wear one too!) the first couple of weeks of school, you can quickly remember those names. It also helps the kids get to know each other's names. (Be prepared for a lot of: "Do we have to wear these stupid name tags?" The answer is "Yes!") There are a lot of books with structured activities that can help you connect with students. (Check out those listed in the bibliography.) If you don't have any books with connecting activities, ask your school counselor. Most counselors are a great resource for these books. Use them! If you don't feel comfortable doing these activities initially, ask your school counselor to help. It is also important to keep doing connecting activities throughout the school year. Frequently educators do a great job connecting the first week and then forget about keeping it up. Once you build a good foundation, maintenance is not hard. But **connections do have to be maintained.**

One key to maintenance is having a way for new students to connect with what is going on in the classroom. We suggest forming a welcoming committee to help new students "connect." To do this, divide the number of students in your class by the number of months you are in school. Put every student's name in a basket and have a student draw the number of names on the welcoming committee that month. In a high school or middle school, do this in home room. You could have a classroom meeting to figure out what would be the task of the welcoming committee. Ask the students if they have ever been the "new kid." How did it feel? Did they like it? What would have helped ease their anxiety? We also advocate that the welcoming committee eat lunch with the new student for at least the first week.

Many times educators are worried that if they connect with students, they lose the ability to maintain discipline in the classroom. The fear is that students will view them as too friendly. This can be avoided if you understand that your job is BOTH to connect and to teach, to be in charge. In other words, you have a job to do. If you have to discipline a student you can simply say, "I am your friend, but my job is to keep the classroom safe. When you throw your books around, it's not safe."✖

✖ See *Restitution: Restructuring School Discipline* by Diane Chelsom Gossen, New View Publications (1993).

# Pat on the Back

I teach first grade at an elementary school. I usually have a class size of between 20 to 22 students. Because I often have transfers in and out of my classroom, I began using connecting activities every two weeks. One activity really stands out, it's called "Pats on the Back."✖

I had no idea what impact this activity would have on one of my students. I did this activity in February. A new student had joined our class about a month earlier. Isabell was a very large, tall girl. When she first came into my room, I was looking beyond her for a younger sister. I guessed that Isabell must belong in the fifth grade. Thank goodness the secretary noticed my mistake and drew my attention toward Isabell.

This child did poorly academically. She was shy and made few friends, according to the paperwork her mother filed. Her family moved frequently, and she had already attended four other schools.

For this activity, I decided that I would pair the students up

✖*Quality Time for Quality Kids.*by Glenn Smith and Kathy Tomberlin. New View Publications (1992).

61

so that they would not be with their best friends. I paired Isabell with one of my quieter girls, who is a small child. Students were asked to make cut-out figures of their hands. Isabell and her partner started talking and working on their project. They made their hands and put them on one another's backs. I was glad to see that Isabell was smiling and talking quite a bit. Then she came to me and showed me her "pat on the back." She was ecstatic.

I told the students that they would then share their pats with the entire class. Isabell was beaming! She showed everyone she met that day what was on her back. She told everyone how her new friend thought that she was nice.

Her partner told her that she liked Isabell because Isabell talked nicely to her and that she was a good friend. From that moment on, Isabell was much more open in the classroom. Her mother came in and told me how much Isabell liked the class and me. She also said that Isabell was working harder on her homework.

I had no idea that this activity would mean so much to anyone. It really opened my eyes to how the children were feeling and to how they engaged in certain activities. I have continued to use more involvement activities that were geared towards getting to know each other and staying connected.

SANDY PAUL
CUMBERLAND COUNTY
(NORTH CAROLINA) SCHOOLS

## PERSONAL GROWTH

One aspect of a positive school climate, according to R.H. Moos, is personal growth and development. In the last decade educators have been asked to use a lot of approaches to personal growth with students. Here is a short list:

* Character Education
* Resiliency Building
* Caring Communities
* Conflict Resolution/Peer Mediation
* Service Learning
* Teacher (or Student) Assisted Programs
* Cooperative Learning
* Adventure Learning/Problem-Based Learning/Challenge Learning
* Student Assistance Teams
* Renaissance

You could probably add others. These programs' effectiveness can all be explained by Perceptual Control Theory because they approach students from the inside out (*the plant view*). They take into account that each person will have his own unique way of behaving. Each helps students grow personally, which then helps to build a more positive school climate.

Another way to help students grow personally is to teach them Perceptual Control Theory and some of its applications. This can be done over the course of the school year and is best achieved by modeling. There are materials that can help you do this. (See the bibliography at the end of the book for materials we recommend.) Because we can't control others, it is imperative that we teach our students as much as we can about how they can control themselves!

## REDEFINING YOUR REFERENCE

A modern educator knows that creating connections with kids is a large part of the job. Our students need role models, and for many of them the adults at school are the most positive role models they have in their lives. More is at stake than the end-of-grade tests. Students who take responsibility for themselves and help those around them will, without a doubt, achieve more and be safer. Educators who take responsibility for connecting with their students will, without a doubt, be happier, achieve more, and be safer.

## REFLECT ON IT!

*It's time to gaze into your reflecting pond. Do you like what you see? Are you being the educator you want to be? Are these statements true for you?*

✱ I provide opportunities for all students to respond in class to critical thinking skills questions.

✱ I give all students adequate wait time when I ask them a question.

✱ I give feedback on student performance as often as possible to all students.

✱ I know my students' names and call them by their names when addressing them.

✱ I take time to get to know each of my students personally.

✱ I take time to let my students know me as a person.

✱ I provide individual help to my students in a friendly manner.

* I use courteous language with all of the students and adults in the building.

* I provide opportunities on a regular basis for students to connect with each other.

A s curriculum coordinator of Kennedy Learning Center, I have been able to see how Perceptual Control Theory has transformed our students during their time with us. Students believe that we do things differently here. I often talk to students about their perceptions about the climate at the center and how that compares to their experiences in other schools. Here is what one of them said:

*"Teachers actually care here. I come to school more here because they know me. It is not easy to stay home when they are involved with you so much. I am more aware of what I do because the teachers are cooperative with me. They try to know me."*

Clearly, the connections that staff have with students are a powerful part of the way we do things here.

ALICE MCGOWAN
WINSTON-SALEM/FORSYTH COUNTY
(NORTH CAROLINA) SCHOOLS

# Lunch Bunches

As a principal of an elementary school, I have been working with my staff introducing the idea of what we want our school to look like. We had a blast envisioning our dream school — which included lots of practical ideas as well as a few pipe dreams. As a result we were able to quickly identify with how helpful this tool of building a common reference could be. We next aimed our sights specifically on our cafeteria.

During our first endeavor to define acceptable cafeteria conduct — discussing things such as restaurant manners, voice levels, cleanliness, and traffic procedures — we became overwhelmed with the details. It dawned on us that something as simple as gathering utensils on a tray could be a disaster if we did not take the time to get our references in sync. At this point, we decided to step back and really define what mattered to us in a cafeteria setting. The data clearly showed that

adults were far more concerned about controlling the environment than our students were. Imagine this: our students thought a cafeteria was a place to eat, converse with friends, talk about kid stuff, and have a short "brain break." Our teachers seemed to focus on the need to maintain control, noise level, cleanliness, and getting students in and out on time. IRK!

Needless to say, our cafeteria consensus-building sessions were the longest and most laborious to date. Step by step, piece by piece, we looked at each activity — from lining up in the hall, securing lunch, cleaning up after oneself, all the way to discussing what our expectations were. Y-charts were hung as reminders everywhere. We had microwave use Y-charts, line-up Y-charts, paying for lunch Y-charts, etc. Sounds controlled doesn't it? But nothing could be further from the truth!

Today we think the cafeteria is a great place to be. After careful examination of our references from every angle, we set about to define what we wanted, how we planned to get there, and what it would require to monitor and make the changes. The first thing we did was to compare what we expected as adults on the rare occasions when we were able to go to lunch with our co-workers. How would it feel to have someone "red-light, green light" us at every turn or reprimand us every time we got loud? As a result, our best option was to teach students to "own" their behaviors in order to "own" the freedom afforded in a cafeteria setting. Our changes surprised us.

The first thing we did was do away with the long tables found in most school cafeterias, our belief being that long tables contributed to louder voices. We replaced them with round tables. We used each table, surrounded by six chairs, to form our "Lunch Bunches." Considering the time constraints of cycling classes through the cafeteria, each class was assigned four tables, allowing us to cycle five classes at a time.

The benefits of this small change snowballed into results beyond our imagination. Students began rotating Lunch Bunch groups on a weekly or monthly basis. This allowed students to build relationships with classmates they might not have otherwise gotten a chance to know. Students experienced first-hand concepts such as diversity and respect. Table manners improved, voice levels decreased, and we found ourselves focusing less on discipline. We now have two adult cafeteria monitors, and teachers no longer have to eat with students as guards, but are free to form their own Lunch Bunches. This year, once students are finished eating they can move to our outside courtyard. Imagine students enjoying these few minutes of freedom until it's time for their teacher to pick them up and escort them to class. No adults! Some even bring a book to read.

**ADELE UPCHURCH**
CUMBERLAND COUNTY
(NORTH CAROLINA) SCHOOLS

# safety

## ASK, DON'T TELL !

I worked in "The Hut" created out of flexible PVC pipe draped with bolts of cloth in primary colors. Right from the beginning I wanted everyone — staff, students, and parents — to know this was going to be a different approach to discipline. "The Hut" became a physically and emotionally safe environment for everyone to self-evaluate and figure out a next step. One of the most gratifying parts of the process was when students reconnected with their teachers and returned to my office to celebrate the learning by stamping their hand *print in ink on the wall of "The Hut" with their name and date. This visual documentation became a powerful way to celebrate the reconnections made between the students and staff. All of this came about when Michael Golden, the principal of a thirteen-hundred-student middle school, called and pleaded, "Come help me. Let's focus on demonstrating to teachers a non-punitive approach to classroom management."*

*I began working with school staff and students at West Middle School in Rockford, Illinois, in 1992. After two years of training teachers and implementing Control Theory concepts with students at West, there was a 40 percent decrease in the number of discipline referrals. Now, eleven years later, the number of discipline referrals has decreased 64 percent. Most remarkable, however, were the academic results of the students I initially worked with. These students were deemed to be the most "at risk." Yet after working with these students on Control Theory concepts, teachers saw an improvement in achievement and an increase in time spent on task in the classroom. Specifically, grade point averages increased 20 percent after implementing these ideas, as compared with the rest of the school's population, which was deemed to be a group of higher achievers.*

*An essential part of this process was developing*

*a **belief statement**, first for the school, and then for the school and community working together:*

***We are a West family committed to achievement with mutual dignity and respect.***

*Parents and community members recognized the importance of improving relations among students, and among students and teachers. As a result, behavior and academics improved. As one parent said: "It's all about relationships."*

– JEFF GRUMLEY

In *A Connected School* we promote a simple idea supported by research: safety equals connectedness. Without safety there is little opportunity for caring or learning to occur, and without caring connections safety can become an issue. A report published in 2002 from the Center for Adolescent Health and Development at the University of Minnesota once again corroborates our thinking: "Most students in most

73

schools across the country feel pretty connected to school. They feel an attachment to their friends and teachers." The report suggests the following in terms of discipline policies: "When schools have harsh or punitive discipline policies, students feel less connected to school. The discipline policy for any particular infraction does not influence connectedness. Rather, a harsh discipline climate in general is what seems to be associated with lower school connectedness."✖

In *Beyond Discipline,* Alfie Kohn makes a strong case to move away from corrective measures such as punishments and rewards and

✖ *Improving the Odds: The Untapped Power of Schools to Improve the Health of Teens* (2002), authored by R.W. Blum, C.A. McNeely, and P.M. Rinehart, was based on analysis of data from the University of North Carolina's Add Health Study.

towards creating caring communities. Kohn describes such caring school communities as places in which students feel cared about and are encouraged to care about each other, where they experience a sense of being valued and respected, where the children matter to one another and to the teachers, where they feel connected to each other, where they are part of an "us." As a result, they feel safe in their classes, not only physically but also emotionally. In spite of the inroads made by Kohn, the fact remains that punishments and rewards are basic building blocks of many school discipline programs. Why don't punishments and rewards work in the long run?

An understanding of Perceptual Control Theory helps us figure this out. Kids are living control systems seeking a dynamic balance between what

they want to happen and what they perceive to be happening. If the reward, the M&M's, stickers, praise, isn't important to them (isn't a reference for what they want to be happening), they will experience "error signals" and move on to something that is important to them.

**REWARDS** ignore internal motivation and focus on an external object. If the student does not want the external object, the reward will not change the behavior.

Rewards only work if (1) students want the external object and (2) students want to comply. If an adult wants a student to comply, the most effective course is simply to ask, "Would you be willing to...?" If the student wants to be respected, a respectful request will be perceived as a reference.

Certainly, asking doesn't work all the time. But at least the minimum is maintained when it doesn't work, namely, a connection with the other person. And this connection may be seen as respect. In PCT terms, the students will experience less error if respect is the focus of what is wanted. In general, respect to any human means no coercion, neither positive (reward) nor negative (punishment).

Early psychology set off on the wrong foot, basing its premise in mechanical physics, external forces impacting inanimate objects, rather than focusing on living control systems.

**A**s a teacher, if you want to move away from punishing and rewarding (attempting to control externally) and towards developing "discipline within" students, what do you do?

You work at it — and keep working at it. One of the first things to do is to understand the model of internal control and purposeful behavior yourself, and then connect it to anything and everything that will help your students understand themselves as living control systems. Alfie Kohn talks about caring communities. Diane Gossen talks about *Restitution*. Fletcher Peacock talks about *Watering the Flowers, Not the Weeds.*

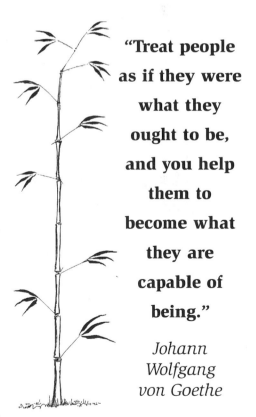

**"Treat people as if they were what they ought to be, and you help them to become what they are capable of being."**

*Johann Wolfgang von Goethe*

Marshall B. Rosenberg talks about *Nonviolent Communication*. Phil Vincent talks about *Developing Character*. Parker Palmer talks about *The Courage to Teach*. All of these ideas can help develop discipline within because they recognize that students are more like plants than rocks. These ideas are grounded in the context of living control systems seeking dynamic balance.

Each of these approaches challenges us to view the situation at a higher level of perception and thus connect to others. This is how we achieve safe schools. Students and staff are disciplining themselves and are learning how to be the best people they can be. Remember that the origin of the word "discipline" is "to learn." In *A Connected School*, discipline means discovering what our references and perceptions are in order to commit to healthy relationships and meaning-

ful activity. Self-discipline, or discipline within, takes students way beyond following rules and conforming to expected behaviors.

**DISCIPLINE WITHIN** establishes a set of **connected references** among everyone in the school by engaging in a process to create a **common picture** of who we want to be individually and how we want to be together.

**A CONNECTED SCHOOL** is a safe environment where students and staff care about each other and care that something meaningful is achieved. It's like building a team. There are players, coaches, managers, owners, sponsors, and hometown fans all operating at different levels (one network within many networks) with one goal in mind — a winning season.

Let's carry the team analogy further and apply it specifically to baseball. Sitting in the catbird seat, bases loaded, two strikes, three balls, a masterful windup, who's thinking about owners or sponsors? The awareness is focused on the drama at hand. At the moment of the pitch, awareness of the crowd, the time of day, the sponsors — all simply fade. Attention is focused on the pitch, the way the pitcher curls his fingers around the ball, the muscular tension in the wrist, arm, shoulder, the release. The same thing happens day after day in schools across the globe. At any given moment our awareness is focused on one and only one thing: the drama at hand. The focus of our attention is often on the drama between the student and the teacher. Not the winning season … achievement and learning. So how could this possibly have anything to do with safety, discipline, and bottom lines?

"Bottom lines" refer to actions that jeopardize the physical and psychological safety of students and staff. "Bottoms lines" often draw our attention because they create large error signals at a high level in school systems. When discussing issues such as harassment, weapons, alcohol, drugs, physical violence, and defiance, the concern focuses on life and death, health and well-being. Through their discipline policies and procedures many educators deal with such situations by screaming, "That's a bottom line! You're out!!"

In *A Connected School*, there are "bottom lines." But we strive to develop discipline within, to have students connect to one another, to staff, and to a larger community. And more often than not, we hope to hear, "YOU'RE SAFE." This can be achieved by working with the students to figure out a better way and specifically to decide what their next steps should be to move them in the right direction.

In *A Connected School*, we believe understanding PCT helps us shift from focusing on behavior at the program level (what the student is doing) to "bumping it up" to the principle level (who is the person I want to be). If you view discipline in this manner, the playing field changes.

**B**retta, a middle school student, tells the story about the day she got in trouble at school. This was a first for her; she had never received any disciplinary referrals before. It was gym class. She had the ball and was deciding where to toss it. Instead of tossing it to one of her friends, she decided "to go the extra mile" (a perceived act of kindness on her part) by throwing it to Jan, someone occasionally left out of the loop. This particular throw was not made with accuracy nor was it caught with skill, and the ball bumped off Jan's glasses. Jan was upset, but neither she nor her glasses were harmed. Nevertheless, the gym teacher accused Bretta of deliberately trying to hurt Jan. Bretta was sent to talk with the principal. By watching the behavior alone, someone might assume, like the gym teacher did, that Bretta intended to harm Jan. But if we understand PCT, we know we have to ask Bretta — only she can speak about what she intended by her action. In this case, she said that she wanted to include Jan instead of just throwing the ball to one of her friends. We would also have to ask Jan about her perceptions, and the teacher as well.

**Students don't always remember what we teach them, but they seldom forget how we treat them.**

*We simply don't know what happened until we understand what each person wanted. What was the "mismatch," the error that each person was trying to reduce?* Perceptual Control Theory helps us understand we are constantly engaged in a process of attempting to maintain a sense of dynamic balance, a match between what we want to be perceiving and what we are perceiving.

Bretta's situation is a classic example of what occurs time and again throughout a typical school day. In changing the playing field you must first examine your beliefs about safety, discipline, and your role in the process. Then remember a principle tenet of *A Connected School*:

## ASK, DON'T TELL!

Let's take a closer look at some common views about safety and discipline:

**View 1:** External control is effective.

**A Connected School View 1:** **Internal control is more satisfying and is how all living systems operate.** Trying to control students from the outside may be the acceptable norm, but if this is not satisfying or valuable to you, what purpose does it really serve? As a middle school principal says, "I'd rather be happy and wrong (focusing on the internal locus of control), than miserable and right (trying to control others)." We are back to questions we have already asked: How much of your day is spent attempting to control others? How effective are you being? Is this what you want to be doing?

**View 2:** Telling students when they have done something wrong builds character.

**A Connected School View 2:** Living systems are designed to pay attention to what isn't working. Therefore, focusing on the positive is essential. People know when they have done something wrong. People may not want to admit it because they want to save face. People naturally want to be perceived as successful. What students may not have encountered is an adult who tells them that they have done something right. How much better it is for students to have a success identity — being acknowledged for what they do well, thinking for themselves, and getting what they want without hurting others. Help students be aware of their own internal error signals so that they can self-regulate.

**View 3:** **Isolation or exclusion is a deterrent for a misbehaving individual.** Teaching is for those who want to learn; discipline is for those who don't want to learn. "I have got to get rid of the bad apple, I've got twenty-eight other students who want to learn."

**A Connected School View 3:** **Involvement or inclusion is an opportunity for others to care for an individual and discover that we are more alike on the inside than different on the outside.** We understand that every living system is always behaving to maintain dynamic balance. Misbehaviors are seen as learning opportunities for both the individual and the group to learn new behaviors for maintaining this dynamic balance. In doing so we decrease the probability of future incidents, thereby, increasing students' abilities to be self-disciplined. Students who understand their own behavior as well as the behavior of others build discipline within themselves to do the right thing when no one else is looking.

# The Lineup

I am a school social worker with Orange County Schools in North Carolina. At one of my schools, I have been working with a nine-year-old boy I'll call John. John has been diagnosed with an anxiety disorder. When he doesn't understand something he calls himself "stupid" and hits himself on the head. On several occasions, when John has had a screaming and crying meltdown, his teacher has had to call for assistance.

Even though John has many difficulties, he has many strengths. He is very sensitive toward other people. He tends to take those who are outcasts under his wing. He is very kind to others and gives a lot of compliments.

John and I have always gotten along. We have a rapport based on trust and acceptance. Sometimes I am called into his class to help him calm down and get back on task. Recently, the class was lining up to go outside and the teacher asked everyone to walk quietly down the hall. The teacher warned that if they couldn't follow the rules, they would not go outside, but the students continued to talk. John loves to go outside, so he started screaming at everyone. I was

called to talk to him.

**Me:** What happened today that upset your teacher?

**John:** I was yelling at other kids because they were being loud.

**Me:** What did you want to accomplish when you started yelling at your classmates?

**John:** I wanted them to be quiet so we could go outside.

**Me:** Help me understand. Your teacher wants everyone to be quiet before going outside?

**John:** Yes, we have to stand in line and be quiet and then we can walk down the hall to the door.

**Me:** Were you following directions?

**John:** I was trying to help make everyone be quiet so we could go outside.

**Me:** By doing what you did, do you think you were following directions?

**John:** (*Shrugging his shoulders*) I guess not. I just wanted to make everyone be quiet.

**Me:** Let me ask you something. Who do you have control over?

**John:** What do you mean?

**Me:** Can you control what other people say?

**John:** No.

**Me:** Can you control what other people do?

**John:** No.

**Me:** Can you control what you say?

**John:** No.

**Me:** You can't control what you say?

**John:** (*Smiling*) Yes, I can.

**Me:** Can you control what you do?

**John:** Yes.

**Me:** Then who do you have control over?

**John:** Myself.

**Me:** Okay, let me ask you again. Were you following your teacher's directions when you and your classmates were standing in line?

**John:** No.

**Me:** Did it help when you yelled at your classmates?

**John:** No.

**Me:** What happened?

**John:** I got into trouble and didn't get to go outside with everybody else.

**Me:** Do you like going outside for recess?

**John:** Yes.

**Me:** So next time when you are lining up to go out for recess, imagine that everyone is being loud and not listening to your teacher. What are you going to do?

**John:** I don't know.

**Me:** Well, let me ask you something. What kind of student do you want to be?

**John:** A good one.

**Me:** What is a good student to you?

**John:** Someone who doesn't get into trouble … someone who does his work.

**Me:** If you did your work to help your classmates get ready to go outside, what would that say about you?

**John:** I'm smart.

**Me:** So what would being smart look like if you wanted to quietly lead your class outside?

**John:** I'd show them.

**Me:** Like how?

**John:** I would be quiet and stand in line facing forward.

**Me:** Even if everyone is being loud?

**John:** Yes, because that way I will be showing everyone how to be quiet.

ELIZABETH ROMSKA
ORANGE COUNTY
(NORTH CAROLINA) SCHOOLS

Our approach to discipline and safety works best if it is based on teaching students to be aware of this natural process of self-regulation, for themselves and in a social context such as school. Our intent is to have teachers model self-evaluation. This is the most powerful way for teachers to teach and students to learn to develop discipline within. It is also imperative that you connect references in your classroom.

How can you connect with your students, and keep connecting, while maintaining a safe environment where meaningful activity and achievement can take place ?

Here are our suggestions:

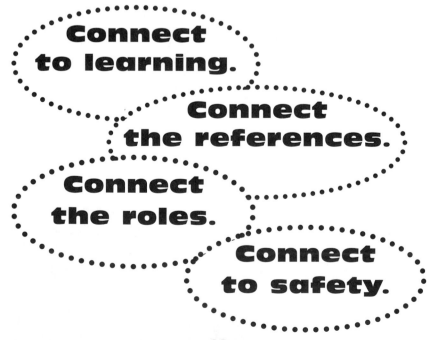

Connect to learning.

Connect the references.

Connect the roles.

Connect to safety.

## CONNECT TO LEARNING

You connect to learning by asking some hard questions about your teaching and your classroom:

* Am I creating a learning environment that is rich in experiences for the students?
* Do I create a learning environment in which students identify their references and evaluate their attempts to create a match?
* Are my lessons multi-sensory and chunked into small enough units?
* Do we celebrate our achievements?

*And a moment of truth ...*
* *Are my lesson plans just plain boring?*

## CONNECT THE REFERENCES

In PCT terms, the "reference" is the individual's intent, goal, purpose, or want. It's something like shadow ball. You can't see references, and they change all the time. We know that a person operates from a multitude of references simultaneously. And the next person operates with another multitude of references. In *A Connected School* students and staff have talked about their intentions, goals, purposes, and wants. They also have a common understanding of their mutual beliefs. These are connected references. You can only connect references by getting to know your students and by them getting to know you.

A way to begin to connect references is through the development of a "belief statement." (This is sometimes referred to as a social contract or class agreement.) Many people confuse belief statements with mission and vision statements, but there are important distinctions. A *vision statement* defines where you want to be, what your goals are for the future. A *mission statement* clarifies the purpose of your class or school. A *belief statement* outlines how we want to be treated and how we want to treat each other while we are accomplishing our vision and our mission.

**BELIEF STATEMENTS bump up our interactions to a higher level by asking, "What do you believe about how you want to be treated and how you want to treat other people?"**

In our work with schools over the last twenty years we have found many educators talking

**reaching HIGHER
becoming STRONGER
making it BETTER
TOGETHER
YES ! YES! YES!**

*– Belief Statement of Haskell
Year-Round Academy
Rockford, Illinois*

about the mission of the school, but few implementing this mission with their students. Judy Anderson, principal of Sheridan Hill Elementary in Richfield, Minnesota, worked with the idea of belief statements when her staff members first implemented the idea of restitution in their school. Teachers were able to foster learning by talking about family or school rules. For example, "no hitting" or "no throwing" are important rules because safety is valued. Thus, safety became part of the school's belief statement.

You can start by creating a belief statement at the staff level and then at the classroom level. Finally, a school-wide belief statement can be created for the entire school community. Done well, it can be fun, exhilarating, and quick! What we have found most effective and successful are belief statements as short summations or jazzy encapsulations. These beliefs capture the spirit of the higher levels of perception and use hand signals to help internalize this knowledge. (Check out the appendix, which walks you through creating a belief statement.)

Margaret Wheatley talks about connected references in terms of creating an invisible field, like the air you breathe, within an organization: "We would do our best to get it permeating through the entire organization so that we could take advantage of its formative properties. ... Anyone who bumped up against it would be influenced by it to create behavior congruent with the organization's goals." The value is in the process of creating it, connecting to create it, and using it to stay connected.

Here are a few ways to use a belief statement to connect students and staff:

* Students and staff record in a daily journal how they "live" their beliefs.
* The statement is posted around the school: letterhead, staff lounge posters, welcome sign, key chains, t-shirts, identification cards.
* At staff meetings, teachers share ways in which they see themselves or others putting their belief statement into action.
* Students are videotaped talking about their

"living" out the belief statement and the tape is shown at faculty meetings.

**If you want to develop discipline within your students, it is essential to talk about beliefs in non-disciplinary situations.** For example, before starting a lesson that involves small group work, ask students: "How do we want to treat each other in our groups today?" At the end of a lesson, day, or week, students can be asked to evaluate their activity guided by their beliefs: "How are we 'reaching HIGHER'?"

## CONNECT THE ROLES

Connecting roles is a way to explore references that students and staff have about their jobs in the school. Connections help students trust in themselves, each other, and their teachers. Diane Gossen has a role clarification exercise called "My Job, Your Job" that is easy and helpful. It can be used between the community and the school, parents and the school, administrators and teachers, teachers and students, teachers and para-professionals, bus drivers and students, or between any two groups who work with one another. The purpose of the activity is to clarify how people see their job and the job of others. It provides a connected reference that can be used to guide self-evaluation.

In the classroom it works something like this: start with some warm-up questions.

* Whose job is it to learn?
* Whose job is it to bring supplies?
* Whose job is it to prepare lessons?

Next, using the information gained from the questions, a list can be made: "It's my job to … and it's your job to …"

A simple way to continue to build connected references is to use these lists to create a new list — "our job" — that clarifies where students' and teachers' jobs overlap.

In the daily routine, if a student isn't on task, the teacher can ask, "What's your job here?" Students know. "Well, can you do your job or do you need some help?" It's a

quick intervention to guide students to self-evaluate and to connect references.

Connecting roles through the "My Job, Your Job" activity is also a way for teachers to understand how students want to be treated. You may find out more than you wanted to know. In high school classes, when asked what the teacher's job was, students have replied: "To treat us right." "Not to talk so much that we can't hear ourselves think." "To teach us something even if we're stupid." "Not to gossip about us with other teachers." In terms of discipline and PCT, when these students perceive that they "aren't being treated right," or they "can't hear themselves think" or they haven't learned anything because they are "stupid," or that teachers gossip about them, they experience an error, a mismatch between what their reference is for teacher behavior and what they perceive to be happening. They then

act on their environment to reduce the error. Teaching students to recognize an error signal and re-evaluate both the reference and the perception teaches them to stay connected and leads to self-discipline.

Organizational development experts have talked for years about the alignment and congruence of three key components for positive morale: goals, roles, and personal strengths. This thinking aligns with the process of connecting the learning, connecting references, connecting roles, and connecting to students, but let's not leave out the main subject of this chapter: safety!

## CONNECT TO SAFETY

The connected safety reference in *A Connected School* is that students have the right to learn in a safe environment, and no student has the right to interfere with the learn-ing and safety of another student. This is a value held by the broader community. At every level in the community, safety is valued. Remember the bottom line, but move beyond it. Bump safety up to the higher levels.

To maintain safety in the context of *A Connected School*, here are some suggestions:

* Talk about and explore safety as a shared value.
* The community, parents, school board, and staff work together to agree on what constitutes reasons to suspend students from school.

* Talk about discipline as "discipline within" and its original meaning, "to learn." "What are the ways we all can learn and all be safe?"
* Parents, staff, and students work together for an explicit understanding of suspension and a reconnecting process.

In *A Connected School* there is a process to help students and teachers reconnect after a suspension. We want to have students who return to classrooms with a clear picture of who they want to be and a new or different reference to control for. We have to work at helping students take baby steps, thinking about the "next step" they can take to become the people they want to be. A student who has a habit of running down the hall and crashing into people won't have an overnight metamorphosis, but we can move the student towards "being a person who pays more attention to others in the hall." Most importantly, remember that connected students are more likely to be self-disciplined because they have connected references. Some ideas for reconnecting include:

✱ Welcoming suspended students back to school through actions and words.

> **Experience is simply the name we give our mistakes.**
>
> *Oscar Wilde*

✱ Providing opportunities to meet with the appropriate staff to discuss options and references and identify small changes that could make a difference.

✱ Figuring out the "next step" needed to reconnect. The "next step" is a small change a student can make to move in a positive direction. This is different from making a plan, because taking these baby steps don't require knowing the final destination in advance.✖

This process allows for students and teachers to maintain a connection, even if students initially

✖ This concept comes from Barnes Boffey.

don't value a caring community. This process offers students an opportunity for service, a way to reconnect. When students voluntarily figure out a better way, they move toward becoming the person they want to be. A success identity emerges. And sometimes dramatic changes occur. Take the example of one alternative high school student, a repeat offender for fighting and violence, who learned to read his own "error signals." He would head for the bathroom, splash cold water all over himself, and then walk down the hall, dripping, saying, "I'm in control. I'm in control."

There is one constant in all of these recommendations for staying connected: we never assume we know what another person is perceiving or wanting. Once again, we hold tightly to a guiding principle of *A Connected School*: "Ask, don't tell."

The goal of "discipline within" is for students to learn to read their own living control system, to know their references or values, to check their perceptions, to evaluate the varying actions they use to create a match between what they want and what they are perceiving, and to learn the value of connecting to others and the larger community. The practice of "discipline within" builds individual character and connection to the community. It creates a concern for the safety and well-being of others. It's a life skill.

Journalist Jay Mathews filed an interesting report in *Newsweek* recently. He wrote about Mike Riley, who as a young teacher in the 1970s tried to "save inner city kids. He found that they blossomed if he simply sat down each day after class and made sure they did their homework. 'They went from F's to honor roll, and I realized that they weren't dumb kids, just kids we hadn't connected to.'" Today, Riley is the superintendent of schools in Bellevue, Washington, designated by *Newsweek* as one of the 100 best high schools in America.

Whatever your beliefs and disciplinary practices have been, there's opportunity for change and improvement. Many of our young people are learning a better way, one that is in keeping with living control systems. As we know from recent brain research, students who feel safe are ready to learn.

## REFLECT ON IT!

*It's time to gaze into your reflecting pond. Do you like what you see? Are you being the educator you want to be? Can you say, "Yes, I do that on a regular basis!" to all of these?*

✱ I frequently evaluate my beliefs and practices by asking: Am I being the kind of person I want to be in this discipline situation? What am I controlling for?

✱ I understand that misbehavior is a person's best attempt to maintain dynamic balance.

✱ When things aren't going well, my students ask themselves, "Am I being the kind of student or person I want to be?"

✱ When talking about or working with a student, I try to understand their references and perceptions by asking, not telling.

✱ I practice teaching by example (modeling) as one of the best ways for my students to learn.

* My students and I have developed a connected reference for how we want to be together.

* I remind myself that building a caring community and helping students develop their own problem-solving skills is essential to my role as teacher.

* When I am out of balance in a discipline situation, I ask myself questions such as: What do I want? Am I being the person I want to be?

# Chill Time

**T**eachers want to know how to create the kind of school environment in which students *want* to learn. At Haskell Year-Round Academy in Rockford, Illinois, where I am principal, we have found several creative ways to accomplish this.

Modeling stability and success is crucial when so many of our students attend the before-school breakfast program (97 percent) and have scored in the bottom quartile on the Stanford Achievement Test. Teachers here want students to shift their reference from past problems and failures to solutions and success.

The staff talks about how to be the kind of teachers we want to be at staff meetings and we post such references in the teachers' lounge. Throughout the day, students are asked, "Are you being the kind of student you want to be?" We want

them to have a clear picture in their minds of "what success looks like."

We also encourage students to ask themselves self-evaluation questions about how they can be successful students.

When an infraction occurs, we say to

students "T.G.I.F," which stands for "Thinking Gets It Fixed." We do not want students to focus on past problems or misbehaviors. Instead, we give students Chill Time to provide them space to think creatively and to focus on higher-level cognitive behaviors. The result: students think about the next step they can take toward becoming the kind of students they want to be.

Teachers also demonstrate discipline within for their students by examining their own behaviors. Recently a teacher raised her voice when talking to a student. She quickly recovered when her student asked her if she needed some Chill Time. She replied, "I wasn't being the kind of teacher I wanted to be when I raised my voice with you."

Here's a similar example: I was attending a meeting so a substitute administrator supervised the playground as I normally would. When two boys got into a fight, he brought them into the principal's office and informed them that they would receive a consequence. But the students insisted, "Mrs. Jacobson lets us chill to see if we can work it out." Even when students receive a consequence based upon our district disciplinary code, we still want them to learn a better way. When students learn how to make it better, we believe they are learning a valuable life skill.

**VICKI JACOBSON**
ROCKFORD (ILLINOIS)
PUBLIC SCHOOLS

# achievement

## BUMP IT UP!

If I wasn't convinced already that schools needed to change, my oldest son Wesley certainly brought the lesson home. Wesley was a very bright, precocious five-year-old. Quick witted, with a vocabulary of about a 10-year-old, and surrounded by educators from the day he was born, he entered the structure of schooling. He was immediately faced with his first struggle to learn some-

*thing — reading. Never before had learning been difficult. Prior to attending school, Wesley could memorize anything and could articulate his inner thoughts and feelings whenever asked. I remember distinctly scheduling an appointment with the psychologist at the local hospital,*

*because Wesley was still doing letter reversals two months into school. The system gave me the typical answer: "He's a boy, he'll grow out of it." Knowing that this was a red flag for this particular child, I didn't wait. I spent the next thirteen years as a parent struggling with the "traditional system" to provide for a child who could read and write at about a fifth-grade level and wanted to take physics and chemistry. Unfortunately, there are thousands of Wesleys out there. I believe we must fundamentally change our reference of what achievement is all about.*

*As I sat down to write this chapter I was faced with a topic that on the surface appears to be simple and direct, only to find that there is neither a simple nor direct way to define "achievement." For many politicians it may have very little to do with learning. It is so complex I encountered one colleague who is planning to write an entire book on the subject. With that in mind I offer here what might be termed "food for thought." I have asked students and educators across the United States and Canada how they define "achievement." The definitions varied widely, but the ones I found most compelling portrayed achievement as both a journey and a destination. I would describe achievement, in terms of PCT, as the gaining of new behaviors that help reduce error. These can be skills, abilities, or knowledge that give individuals ways to maintain dynamic balance, thus allowing an individual to better deal with a more complex world.*

— SHELLEY ROY

In this chapter we will take a closer look at what educators see as the three cornerstones of learning — **curriculum**, **assessment**, and **instruction** — through the lens of PCT. Like the three vertices of an equilateral triangle, curriculum, assessment, and instruction need to be aligned, each carrying its own weight. Each supports the other like the warp and woof of a tapestry of growth and learning.

The term "**curriculum**" is used to describe the *what* of teaching and learning. It has over the past decades taken the form of behavioral objectives, goals, outcomes, and most recently standards. Education has moved far beyond The Three R's: reading, writing, and arithmetic. An interesting side note here comes from a colleague of ours, Lloyd Klinedinst: "The term 'curriculum' comes from the Latin word for running, course, race, a race-ground, career. It is not unrelated to the Latin word for circus, which is a circled or enclosed space for games and athletic contests. ... So for me the term 'curriculum' as it is most commonly

> **"The problem is that the kind of mastery required for students to earn school credits, grades, and high scores on tests is often considered trivial, contrived, and meaningless — by both students and adults."**
>
> *Fred Newmann, Walter Secada, & Gary Wehlage*

used places limits on learning."

"**Assessment**" is the *measurement* of learning and should directly correlate to both the curriculum and the instruction. We should measure learning by the way in which it was taught — what is often described as seamless or embedded assessment. In such a scenario, an observer of a classroom would not be able to tell if you were teaching or assessing. Assessment specialists recommend that we distinguish between assessment and evaluation, assessment being the gathering of data and evaluation constituting a judgement. For educators today these two terms have become blurred. Assessment of learning has been a topic of great discussion among politicians, researchers, and educators over the past decade. This topic has come to the forefront in the United States with the "No Child Left Behind" legislation. Assessment has taken many forms through the years: Paper-and-pencil assessments include multiple choice tests, true-false tests, teacher-designed tests, and standardized achievement tests. Alternative assessments include portfolios, demonstrations, and assessment packages that can be a combination of all of these and other forms of assessment.

"**Instruction**" is the *how* of teaching and describes the way in which educators teach. Over the last decade as new technology has allowed us to glimpse the inner-workings of the brain, educators have been flooded with information on effective instructional strategies. As educators, understanding PCT helps us filter all of these developments in curriculum, assessment, and instruction and spend our time wisely for the greatest chance of success.

## CURRICULUM FOR THE 21ST CENTURY

In the chapter on Perceptual Control Theory we talked about the fact that each of us has billions of our own unique references. In the chapter on safety we discussed the importance of developing connected references for how we want to be with each other. We also talked about "bumping it up," operating from the higher levels of perception rather than from lower levels. All three of these ideas should be taken into account when we think about curriculum in *A Connected School*.

The work of Renate Nummela Caine, Geoffrey Caine, and Sam Crowell in the area of the brain and Jacqueline Brooks and Martin Brooks's✖ work on Constructivism are shifting us away from what can be termed *static knowledge* and moving us toward *dynamic knowledge*. Constructivism is a theory about knowledge and learning based on the premise that each individual learner creates his or her own meaning.

✖ *Making Connections: Teaching and the Human Brain* by Renate Nummela Caine and Geoffrey Caine. ASCD, Alexandria, Virginia. (1991).

*Mindshifts* by Renate Nummela Caine, Geoffrey Caine, and Sam Crowell. Xzephyr Press, Tuscon, Arizona (1994)

*The Case for Constructivist Classrooms* by Jacqueline Brooks and Martin Brooks. ASCD, Alexandria, Virginia. (1993).

This shift aligns well with what we understand about Perceptual Control Theory. Dynamic knowledge allows for the learner to take multiple paths to the same solution. PCT tells us that living systems are designed to use variable means to achieve the same results. The teacher who understands Constructivism understands that each learner has unique references from which they are operating and that each learner will create their own personal meaning. Problem-centered curricula (those that allow critical thinking, the construction of knowledge, and consideration of alternatives) are one of the cornerstones of *A Connected School*. Such curricula also have value beyond the school walls.

In terms of teaching and learning we talk about our connected references as a scope and sequence or an articulated curriculum. Developing connected references for what we should teach is not an easy task. It involves students, teachers, parents, the public, and the politicians. Today the public and political arenas are attempting to develop connected references for what "should be taught" through the development of state standards.

At the same time, the more educators understand about the process of learning, the definition of what's worth teaching has been expanding. What was once thought of as intelligence is expanding. Howard Gardner's work on multiple intelligences and the work of Debra Pickering and Robert Marzano on dimensions of learning are examples of broadening the definition.✖ With the onset of global communication and the availability of information at our fingertips, the amount of knowledge available today is colossal.

✖ *Frames of Mind: The Theory of Multiple Intelligences* by Howard Gardner. Basic Books, Cambridge, Massachusetts (1983).

*Dimensions of Learning* by Debra Pickering, Robert Marzano, Daisy E. Arredondo, Guy J. Blackburn, Ronald S. Brandt and Cerylle A, Moffett. ASCD, Alexandria, Virginia, and Mid-Continent Regional Educational Laboratory, Aurora, Colorado (1992).

**In terms of Perceptual Control Theory, broadening the definition of learning has provided us with more opportunities to "bump it up."**

We can move away from teaching at the sequence and program levels toward teaching at the principles level. This moves us from teaching minute pieces of information and algorithms — static knowledge bound by time and place — to conceptual understanding and problem solving,

**It takes TWO to TEACH — both the instructor and the student must participate!**

which leads to critical thinking and a deeper understanding.

When we bump up the curriculum, we also increase the chance that learners will value what we are trying to teach. If students have a "reference" for what we are trying to teach — if students see how learning this will help them — learning is more likely to occur.

In the United States today, more than half of the states have developed and adopted statewide standards. Take heart if you are a teacher in one of these states and you want to continue to align your practices to PCT.

**Remember that Perceptual Control Theory is nature's way of operating.** When we learn naturally we don't learn chunks of unrelated information. Thematic instruction based on major concepts can be a bridge in *A Connected School*. Take your state or district standards and lay them out. See if you can identify some big themes or connections among the standards. Group them into conceptual chunks. Thematic units are most effective when they are grouped across disciplines. For example, one school laid out the fifth-grade standards in math, reading, science, and social studies. When we asked, "What are some of the big ideas that appear across several of the standards?" themes began to emerge. One repeating concept was "systems." At this grade level, students were exploring number systems, solar systems, and governmental systems. By looking at the standards in this way, teachers had "bumped it up" and moved away from static knowledge. They had moved their reference for curricula to a higher level and could more easily begin to design assessments and instruction around the big idea of systems. If you want help looking at standards in this way, check out the work of Heidi Hayes Jacobs in developing essential questions and Susan Kovalick with integrated thematic instruction.✖

**We see them come,**

**We see them go.**

**Some are fast,**

**Some are slow,**

**Some are high,**

**Some are low.**

**Not a one is like another.**

**Don't ask us why,**

**Go ask your mother.**

*Dr. Seuss*

✖ *Mapping the Big Picture: Integrating Curriculum and Assessment K-12* by Heidi Hayes Jacobs. ASCD, Alexandria, Virginia (1997).

*Exceeding Expectations: A User's Guide to Implementing Brain Research in the Classroom, 2nd Edition* by Susan Kovalik and Karen Olsen. Books for Educators, Covington, Washington (2003).

# We get what we measure.

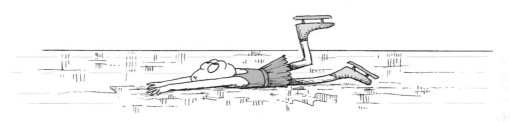

When it comes to measurement, remember that living systems operate based on their own feedback loops. We are naturally designed to constantly monitor what is and what is not working for us. Another core idea linked to PCT and measurement is that we are designed to use variable means to create the same results. The good news for those of us who understand PCT is that the educational tango between achievement and its measurability has led to the development of alternative ways to measure learning. Over the past several years educators have been asked to develop performance assessments that include portfolios, demonstrations, and projects. These methods are internal and unique to each individual and have complex multiple answers, allowing for variable means to the same result (*the plant view*). At the same time the public has been asking for more rote recall, paper-and-pencil testing, and standardized tests. These methods are external and do not take into account individuality. They are, in fact, designed to "sort" students (*the rock view*). Sorting allows some students to rise to the top and others to sink to the bottom.

Measurability requires both storage and retrieval. We often ask students to learn the steps and be able to perform the steps at any given time, even if they have no interest in the topic. Taking what we now know about human behavior, we know that inviting the learner to partner in the process is much more effective. We can do this by individualizing instruction in the class-

**Invite the learner to partner in the process of learning the steps.**

room and by conducting student-led conferencing. Such conferences allow students to set their own individual "references" for achievement and take advantage of their own feedback loops, allowing students to process what's working and what's not working for them. Putting the learner first in the process has led many school systems to implement measuring systems that move measurability to the level of the individual learner. Growth assessments, such as the Norwest Achievement Level Test, measure the growth of an individual learner over a year's time. This form of assessment is beginning to show that learners who traditionally score poorly on standardized tests (usually minority students or students coming from lower socio-economic levels) are making greater gains in one year than students who score at or above the magic fiftieth percentile on standardized tests. This is a classic example of Perceptual Control Theory in action. When we use the natural feedback system of the individual, we make greater gains.

Thus, if you truly want to measure a child's achievement, find creative ways to measure individual talents and growth of the system as a whole. As politicians attempt to create a "one size fits all" way of measuring achievement and researchers try to expand how we measure achievement, *A Connected School* must provide both an answer to the public for how well the schools are doing and an answer to the students about their individual progress. Therefore, we need multiple achievement measures. We must connect references by asking,

## What constitutes learning and how will learning be measured?

To align with PCT, the answers to this question should be:

* **broad**, not narrow,
* **complex**, not simple, and
* **flexible** resolutions, not single answers.

PCT teaches us that having a connected reference creates less error and helps keep the system in dynamic balance. PCT also teaches us that what we look for (control for) is what we pay attention to. Simply put, we get what we expect! But when we don't agree on what we expect, no one gets what they want.

## ORCHESTRATE THE LEARNING

A critical question in aligning behavior to an understanding of PCT is: "What can I control?" Of all of the roles today's educators are asked to play, the actual art of teaching is the one

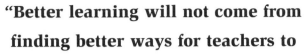

"Better learning will not come from finding better ways for teachers to instruct, but from giving the learner better opportunities to CONSTRUCT."

*Seymour Papert*

where the educator has the most control. I have heard "educators" described as a group of independent contractors each working off of a different blueprint. If a clear reference is drawn (a blue print of what we want and how we will measure it), then collectively the independent contractors can create a magnificent work of art. This is exactly what we want in *A Connected School*.

Like everything involving living control systems, instruction is a balancing act, starting with some but not too much error. If we have no error we see no reason to learn; if our systems have too much error we can't learn. Thus a positive climate in which learning takes place is essential, rather like having fertile ground in which to grow plants. Strive to create cognitive dissonance in a safe place.

Next, try to balance the student's present level of understanding with the desired level. Liv Vygotsky talked about this in terms of the zone of proximal development. We call it the "bubble" theory. The image we have of the students is that each of them has a present "set of references" (knowledge or skill about a subject), much like the bubble that surrounded Glinda the Good Witch in *The Wizard of Oz*. As teachers, our job is two-fold. First, find out what's in the bubble and, second, pitch the lesson close to the bubble without popping it. If we pitch the lesson inside the bubble, learners are bored. If we pitch the lesson too far from the edge of the bub-

**For learning to take place, we want some but not too much error.**

ble, they are frustrated. The goal, in PCT terms, is enough but not too much error. Error steers behavior. In layman's terms, error creates the desire to learn.

It is important to maintain this dynamic balance throughout the learning process. One way to do this is using a technique recommended by Eric Jensen, a recognized leader in brain-compatible instruction. He calls the technique a Novelty Sandwich. This is a pattern for instructional design in which the new learning (novelty) is sandwiched between the buns (ritual).

> **"A person in error was a person searching for the truth."**
>
> *John Lienhard*

Remember that each individual operates based on his own unique perceptual system. We all sit in the same meeting, and we all hear something different. Rita Dunn, Bernice McCarthy, and Anthony Gregorc have all provided models for teaching to these multiple perceptual systems through their work on learning styles and teaching multiple modalities. The secret here is to understand that as a teacher you have a better chance of the lesson reaching the student if it is provided through a sensory-rich real-life experience. Rather like natural learning, it involves all of our senses: tactile, kinesthetic, auditory, and visual. It also taps into all types of mental processes: abstract, concrete, random, and sequential. Some researchers call this type of teaching "orchestrated immersion."✖

✖ See the following materials:

*Teaching Students Through Their Individual Learning Styles: A Practical Approach* by Rita Dunn & Kenneth Dunn. Reston Publishing, Reston, Virginia (1978).

*Using the 4MAT System to Bring Learning Styles to Schools* by Bernice McCarthy in *Educational Leadership* 48, pages 31-37.

*An Adult's Guide to Style* by Anthony Gregorc. For information, see www.gregorc.com/

*Experiential Learning: Experience as the Source of Learning and Development* by David A. Kolb. Prentice-Hall, Englewood Cliffs, New Jersey (1984).

**When you ORCHESTRATE learning, involve all of the senses: tactile, kinesthetic, auditory, and visual. Also tap into all types of mental processes: abstract, concrete, random, and sequential.**

**D**uring instruction don't forget another core concept of Perceptual Control Theory:

## THE FEEDBACK LOOP

You do this in a classroom through **reflection** (self-evaluation) and **metacognition** (thinking about thinking). Keep in mind that students learn through their own internal feedback. Outside sources can be perceived as disturbance. "Disturbance" is anything in the environment that keeps us from getting what we want. Unfortunately, often when teachers try to provide students with feedback, it is taken in as disturbance by the learner. A classic example of disturbance in the classroom is "noise." We are constantly monitoring the noise level in a classroom setting. The noise level at any given time is basically feedback. When in the middle of the lesson the principal comes over the loudspeaker, we perceive this as disturbance. It interferes with our teaching (what we want). When we act as a participant and guide on the journey of learning, we have a better chance of being perceived as feedback for the students, rather than disturbance.

So what is an effective instructional sequence?

Here is a broad example of an instructional sequence that takes into account current educational strategies and Perceptual Control Theory.

| TEACHING STRATEGY | PCT CONCEPT |
|---|---|
| **Jumpstart Your Thinking** | **✳ Check out present references for the material.** What do students already know? This is sometimes called an anticipatory set. |
| **Create a Question** Essential questions steer the learning process. | **✳ Creating a question creates a difference between what I know and what I want to know, in PCT terms "error."** Have learners develop key questions for the lesson that they hope to have answered. |
| **Anchor Activities** | **✳ The more natural the learning experience and the more input provided, the better chance that students are paying attention.** Have students experience activities that use as many senses as possible, are complex, and are similar to what they may encounter outside of school. |
| **Reflection/ Metacogniton** | **✳ Remember that living control systems are made up of millions of feedback loops.** Have students process not only the content, but also how they understand the content and how they learned the content. |

You are probably already familiar with several processes for Reflection/Metacognition. One frequently used is called "KWL," a process that allows for both creating a question within the students and reflective practice throughout the process. Students start by drawing three columns on a sheet of blank paper. They then fill in the first column marked "K" with what they already KNOW. Then they fill in the second column "W" with what they WANT to know. The last column "L" is filled in with what they have LEARNED about the topic or subject. The sheet can be used as an ongoing guide to personal learning. We often add a twist at the end and ask learners to write a new question about what they want to know next. This helps to convey the idea that the process of learning never ends and only creates more questions.

Jumpstart Your

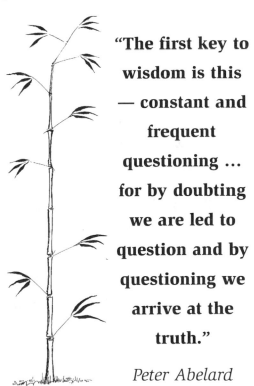

"The first key to wisdom is this — constant and frequent questioning ... for by doubting we are led to question and by questioning we arrive at the truth."

*Peter Abelard*

Thinking and Anchor Activities are also concepts you are probably familiar with. Using these strategies, the teacher gets learners ready and thinking about the subject. This can be done with stories, jokes, experiments, or quotes. In terms of PCT, this accomplishes two things: first we can monitor the present references the learner has, and second we create a small amount of error in the system to naturally steer learning.

Anchor Activities build on the brain's natural ability to retain and recall vast amounts of information stored as episodic memory. The classic Anchor Activity would be a field trip. The best Anchor Activities can be revisited time and again and deeper and deeper meaning can be drawn from them. Anchor Activities go to the heart of PCT because they are self-directed.

In their book *In Search of Understanding: The Case for Constructivist Classrooms*, Jacqueline Grennon Brooks and Martin Brooks define Constructivism as the learner taking responsibility for her own learning. They outline five principles of Constructivist teaching:

* Posing problems of emerging relevance to the learner.
* Structuring learning around primary concepts. Organizing information around conceptual

**WHO'S LEADING WHOM?**
**In A CONNECTED SCHOOL,**
**the learning is directed**
**by the learner.**

clusters of problems, questions, and discrepant situations.

✱ Seeking and valuing the learners' points of view.

✱ Adapting curriculum to address the learners' suppositions.

✱ Assessing learning in the context of teaching, sometimes called *seamless assessment*.

Anchor Activities are by their nature designed to be Constructivist, where the learning is directed by the learner.

# Life Lessons

As I reflect back on my years as a public school teacher, many changes have taken place both in how I structure my classroom and how I design my lessons. Perceptual Control Theory has played a part in these changes.

A few years ago, the position of teaching fifth-grade science opened up. No one on the fifth-grade team "stepped up to the plate." In other words, everyone else refused to teach this subject matter. So I accepted the challenge.

A science lesson in my classroom today looks and sounds very different than this same lesson would have several years ago. Each lesson now begins with a "question of the day." This question can take different forms — it might be a review or it might be science trivia. Whatever form it takes, it helps the students jump into "thinking about science."

Then I proceed with the rest of the science lesson. I also make sure that lessons are based on multiple modes of learning: audito-

ry, visual, kinesthetic, and tactile. Here is a specific example of a fifth-grade science lesson on static electricity:

We began with the "question of the day": *Name a time in your life that you experienced static electricity.* Students were encouraged to share their answers, right or wrong.

Then I moved into a vocabulary section. Three key vocabulary words were presented, and students were asked to identify where they would put these words on a chart I had created. The chart had three columns labeled *I Know I Know*, *I Think I Know*, and *I Know I Don't Know*. We made a large class chart on the black board and used post-it notes. Students also had their own charts in their science journals. At a glance, I could then see which of the vocabulary words the students were familiar with and which were new to them.

Next I told the students about the materials they would use in their static electricity experiments. As a whole-class activity, I had them prepare a graphic organizer in their journals for parts of the experiment. Students were then given time to explore and discover what would happen with their experiments. They then recorded their findings in their journal pages in the appropriate spaces. The last box of their graphic organizers was reserved for students to reflect on what they learned that day.

**SUE SAUER**
REINBECK COMMUNITY
(IOWA) SCHOOLS

"You cannot teach
a person anything.
You can only help them
discover it within themselves."
*Galileo*

**T**his chapter was intended to tickle your thinking about the three cornerstones of learning and how research in each of these areas aligns to Perceptual Control Theory. The hope is that by understanding PCT, what you teach, how you teach, and how you measure learning can be more successful. High achievement aligned to PCT requires:

* The curriculum (the *what* of teaching) to be at a high level, to be concept driven, and to connect references across the school community.

* Assessment (the *measurement* of learning) to be Constructivist in nature and involve multiple answers to complex problems (dynamic not static).

* Instruction (the *how* of teaching) to take into account that learning is a complex process of internally creating and revising patterns (references).

For you, the classroom teacher, it is crucial to remember that achievement is impacted moment-by-moment, experienced individually, and usually measured collectively.

## REFLECT ON IT!

*It's time to gaze into your reflecting pond. Do you like what you see? Are you being the educator you want to be?*

* Do you allow for learner-driven exploration?

* Do you assess students' present understanding and prior knowledge?

* Do you "bump it up" by asking students to question their principles or key concepts of how the world operates (rather than lower level memorization of static knowledge at the sequence and program levels)?

* Do your lessons lend themselves to holistic learning (multi-sensory, multi-modality, complex problem solving)?

* Do you rely on the use of the students' internal feedback systems?

* Do you create cognitive dissonance at the next level of understanding for the individual student?

* Do you decrease error in the system (put the student in a state ready for learning) in order to access flexibility of understanding?

Lincoln Elementary is located in Cedar Falls, Iowa. We have approximately 400 students, 25 percent of whom participate in the free- and reduced-lunch program.

Every couple of years we participate in the Harris Survey, which polls students, teachers, and parents about school climate. In a survey conducted five years ago, one major theme stood out: the large amount of time spent on managing student behavior. The data showed that 50 percent of teachers indicated a problem with student behavior. Teachers and staff felt we needed to start doing things differently.

Thus began our journey of learning Perceptual Control Theory and applying PCT principles in our school. The first step was for our entire staff to participate in a four-day PCT workshop. Now, more than 50 percent of our staff have participated in a second, more advanced PCT workshop. Each class develops a belief statement at the beginning of the school year. We also include our school's belief statement each morning with announcements.

Two years ago the Harris Survey was administered again. The percentage of staff who indicated a problem with student behavior decreased to 10 percent. What does all this have to do with academic achievement? We think the answer is "a lot." Teachers believe that applying PCT principles in their own lives and in their classrooms have correlated with their students' higher achievements. Our school's scores on achievement tests continue to increase. And, in fact, last year we scored highest in the district.

**ANDREA CHRISTOPHER**
COUNSELOR, LINCOLN ELEMENTARY
CEDAR FALLS, IOWA

# Lit Connection

**S**everal years ago, my husband, who did not enjoy reading in school, asked me why kids had to read literature. I told him that I use literature as a way to explore ideas about life. My husband's question helped me realize that many of my middle school students might share his teenage perspective on literature. Let's face it: some kids would rather watch paint dry than read a book! When I began to learn about PCT, I realized that my students had few references to connect to reading literature. To help students make this connection, I decided to focus on our independent reading program first.

In our department's independent reading program students are given several annotated booklists and asked to choose novels to read.

Once they have selected their books, students are asked to name two expectations they have of the books prior to reading them. After completing the books, they are asked to explain whether those expectations were met and to provide evidence from the stories to support their answers. Students are then

asked to think about themes implied in the novels. In addition, students evaluate the books and decide whether they would recommend them to others, and if so, to whom and why.

To bump it up another notch, students select two questions from a list of twenty, and prepare fully developed answers for a book talk session led by an adult volunteer facilitator. The small group session allows students to share their ideas, ask one another questions, make recommendations, and hear about titles or authors that might appeal to them. Adult volunteers are asked to share their own enthusiasm for reading and to talk about their favorite books. All of the discussion questions are designed to expand students' thinking about the story. For example: In what ways are you like any of the characters you've read about? Have you changed after reading this book? What connections are there between this book and your own life? What questions do you have after reading this book?

My overriding goals are to help kids enjoy literature and recognize its usefulness in their own lives. Would they want to have an employer, friend, date, or life partner who has some of the qualities of a particular main character? Or are those character's qualities undesirable? Does the plot reflect the experience of the reader? Does it reflect any current issues that confront our world? As you were reading, what were you thinking? Did you make any connections? I want my students to think that reading is time well spent.

As a teacher, this bumping it up to a higher level has allowed me to help students better define references for "who they want to be," and get connected to reading, to each other, and to me as their teacher.

ROSEMARY DALEY
EDEN PRAIRIE
(MINNESOTA) SCHOOLS

# conclusion

## CONNECT! CONNECT! CONNECT!

The purpose of this book is to underpin what educational experts know constitutes a successful school. We hope that by connecting caring, safety, and achievement to a scientific theory, teachers can change not only their schools' practices or climate, but also the culture.

We believe that like a pebble thrown into a pond, understanding PCT can start as a ripple that travels throughout the system and becomes reflected in every interaction. A school culture based on Perceptual Control Theory can dramatically affect the way school administrators make

decisions, teachers conduct day-to-day operations, and all individuals in the school connect moment by moment.

Research shows that successful organizations are anchored by strong belief systems that act as a guide over the life of the organization. These belief systems are most visible during times of crisis. Peggy Odell Gonder and Donald Hymes, who have studied successful organizations, have found five common elements that contribute to the dynamism of a system's culture.

**1** Strongly held beliefs and values.

**2** Stories that communicate what the organization stands for.

**3** Heroes whose actions and accomplishments embody those values.

**4** Rituals and ceremonies that set the tone and reinforce values.

**5** Key individuals who communicate the values to others, through both word and action.

In *A Connected School*, we suggest that the culture of schools be based on key ideas of Perceptual Control Theory:

* Living control systems are constantly attempting to achieve dynamic balance.
* Living control systems have the ability to coexist with other systems.
* Living control system are naturally designed to look for where the system is out of balance and try to lessen the imbalance.
* The higher levels of perception set the references for the lower levels.
* Living control system operate based on circular causality, not linear cause and effect.

We believe that when school leaders align their practices to these ideas they set the groundwork for students to be better connected to the school community, to be better able to find discipline within, and to be motivated to achieve beyond our wildest dreams.

If this seems a daunting task to you, start slowly, making connections one at a time, as oppor-

tunities arise. Psychologist Bill Pollack, a Secret Service consultant working with the U.S. Department of Education, put it simply and succinctly: "There is no secret to being a good, connected teacher. Everyone knows what it is. It's listening and knowing what your students feel. If you know what your students feel, there won't be school shootings, and there won't be boys and girls of desperation. It isn't rocket science.

## "It's connection, connection, connection!"✖

✖ "To Stop a Massacre," *60 Minutes II*, which aired on May 15, 2002.

# appendix

*How to build a Belief Statement
with a Beliefs Bash*

reaching HIGHER
becoming STRONGER
making it BETTER
TOGETHER
YES! YES! YES!

*– Belief Statement of Haskell Year-Round Academy
Rockford, Illinois*

## Background to the Beliefs Bash

Creating a staff belief statement is a way for staff to model how we want to be together. In Perceptual Control Theory terms, we are creating connected references, or what Alfie Kohn calls "a caring community." Children learn from what adults do as well as from what they say. "How we agree to be together" is part of our personal and collective interactions as social beings. The Beliefs

Bash makes explicit what normally is an implicit understanding. Our beliefs inform our decisions about how we agree to be together.

However, we live in an often violent society with punishment and coercion built into the fabric of our institutions. How do we account for the punitive way we have agreed to be together? The answer, although more complex than explained here, is *the rock view* of understanding.

The limitations of a punitive system need to be acknowledged in both our personal and professional lives. We rarely "get it right" the first or second time we attempt new behaviors. Why would we have unrealistic expectations for students who have less experience and knowledge? Several attempts might be needed before we're able to "get it right."

**The Beliefs Bash is about how we want to treat each other and who we want to be together.**

# Do the Beliefs Bash
## (The Process Described)

**1. Family beliefs.** Each participant writes at least three of his or her own family beliefs in silence. *2-4 minutes.*

Ask people to be honest. They may write their family's beliefs as they perceive and understand them to be. This is both a personal and familial understanding of beliefs. If people do not agree with their family's beliefs, they can list their own personal beliefs.

Attempt to "keep things moving" from step #1 to step #8 without getting stuck or bogged down in any one step. The workshop leader should try to model how to behave based upon our beliefs. Remember to bump it up by examining behaviors (looking at "what we do" or the program level) and seeking to understand their importance at a higher level of perception ("Who do I want to be?" and "Why is it important?" at the principle level and systems level).

Remember, there will be time during the Beliefs Bash activity to add to the list of family beliefs or alter the final product. This is a working document, not something etched in stone.

**2. Share beliefs in small groups.** Seek to understand what others value. *6-8 minutes.*

It is important in this step to keep things moving. Share one of your beliefs, and then move on to the next person. After sharing a belief, you might briefly explain why it is important to you. For example: punctuality. "This is important to me and to my family because my father never missed a day of work in thirty-seven years, and as a child I did not miss any days of school for twelve years."

Listening is an important aspect to this step, especially because people are sharing what they value. Those who are listening have the job to "seek to understand" why the stated belief is important to the speaker.

**3. Identify common beliefs in small groups.** Write common beliefs on a separate sheet of paper. The purpose is to find agreed-upon beliefs within the small groups. *4-6 minutes.*

When coming up with common beliefs in the small group it is important to write this new list on a separate sheet of paper. This allows for a natural selection of the most common beliefs, and excludes any beliefs that might be so extreme that there would be individual or group discomfort. There will be time, however, for both an explanation of different beliefs, and a way to include them if necessary, while not disrupting the overall intent of inclusion and working together.

Brevity is best. One or two words give the flavor of the intent behind the belief. There will be ample time in subsequent staff meetings to "unpack" what each word means. The final outcome of a staff belief statement may be reviewed, edited, or revised for several months to be sure that the most important beliefs are included.

**4. Create names for each small group.** Everyone stand and remain in small

groups. Discuss zany names. Once your group has selected a name, sit down to signify to the others that you have made your selection. *2-3 minutes.*

Creating names for the small groups is a quick way to engage participants in a whole-brain activity (following the research about brain dominance theory and learning). The names are listed on a page of flipchart paper for reference during  the next step. Here are some examples: a group of English teachers called themselves the "Wild Wordsmiths" and another group of mostly women teachers named themselves "Four Babes and a Boy." Remember, the zanier, the better.

5. **Create a beliefs list in large groups.** By name, ask each group to share one belief, write it on a large sheet of paper, and continue until each group's list is exhausted. *4-6 minutes.*

The facilitator asks each group, one at a

time, to offer one of their common beliefs (from step #3). A participant who serves as the recorder will write the list of beliefs on a large sheet of clean paper. Each small group calls out one of its beliefs when asked by the facilitator. It is important to write the beliefs as stated by the respective group members. Note that using their words models for them how they should facilitate the process in their classes, using the students' words.

**6. Create a belief statement.** The goal of this step is to (A) select four words (beliefs) from the list and (B) create a belief statement from the selected words. This is a two-step process. *5 minutes, concurrent with step #7.*

**Step A:** Volunteers from each group should select four beliefs from the list. Remember "process vs. product." This means that the focus is on trusting your intuition. Relax and hold the marker in your non-dominant hand. Take a few deep breaths, and tell yourself "I am going to act in the interest of the common good." Open your eyes. Now, as the group leader counts to three, scan the beliefs list and select one belief that "speaks to you" and represents the entire group.

Step A involves a scribe from each of the

small groups. If there are more than four scribes, we suggest that four people stand in front of the beliefs list and make their selections. The additional scribes act as "consultants" who assist if there are problems.

**Step B:** Create a working belief statement. The scribes then create a belief statement, preferably using only four words, but absolutely no more than ten words. Scribes should also create hand gestures or body movements for each word.

Step B is the creation of a four-word statement, either "as is" or used in a sentence. For example, one group selected the words *fun*, *spirituality*, *education*, and *family*. The consultant wrote "Keep It Fun" as the summary statement. The rest of the group nodded in agreement, but didn't know how to include the three other selected words. Adapting to the moment, we decided to check out the new statement. "If we as a staff choose 'Keep It Fun' as our belief statement, what would we be saying to each other?

What would we be doing with each other? What would we be thinking about each other? If we were having fun, we'd be living up to our *faith*. *Education* is fun, too. Sometimes we are too serious in our families, so the goal of having fun brings us *balance*." They then incorporated previous words selected from the beliefs list and combined them with the "Keep It Fun" summation.

The final responsibility of step B is to put hand gestures or body movements to each key word. The scribes will demonstrate the movements and unveil the belief statement to the larger group of participants in step #8.

**7. Get moving.** The rhythm and blues section of the group (this includes all members except the scribes) create a four-beat dance and hand movement arrangement while the scribes complete their exercise (step #6). This will be the prelude and postlude of the Beliefs Bash. *5 minutes, concurrent with step #6.*

You may want to move this larger group of people to a more spacious room (cafeteria or gymnasium) or outside the building where they can move around and not disturb the scribes.

## 8. Celebrate the learning!

**If it's worth learning, it's worth celebrating.**

All participants get in a circle (or whatever arrangement the rhythm and blues section directs) to first provide a prelude dance and hand movements, then the middle section with the belief statement and hand movements, then a postlude dance and hand movements identical to the prelude. Practice once, then do the Belief Bash! *3 minutes.*

The Beliefs Bash activity is a creative, team-building process that can be transformational for groups seeking an identity around their highest values or system of beliefs. Just remember that when conducting the Beliefs Bash, the focus should be more on the process and less on the product. The brain likes visual, auditory, and kinesthetic ways of learning. Activities need to be innovative, ritualized, and challenging.

It will also be helpful if several staff members have implemented components of *A Connected School* in their classrooms and throughout the school community, such as with other staff members, bus drivers, and parents. Going slowly with this approach enhances the journey. We begin with understanding Perceptual Control Theory because we've found that how a school begins to implement change is often where they end. The destination is determined by the way one departs on a journey.

We have seen this Beliefs Bash activity become ineffective when people quibble over words or get hung up on one part of the process. Trust in the desired outcome, and look for agreement among various statements. The goal is to use the belief statement daily, in non-confrontational and non-disciplinary situations so that our experiences may be shared, valued, and used as a foundation for further growth and learning.

## When in Doubt, Clarify and Discuss

When there is disagreement among participants over a particular belief or several beliefs, you may want to include an additional step. It is important to follow this step just as described. Start by asking, "Are there any disagreements, differences of opinion, or need for explanation about any of the beliefs listed on the flipchart?" Place a line before the belief in question. (This line will get a check once the belief is discussed as a group.) Ask the question again:

### "Are there any other beliefs listed here that you want to clarify or discuss?"

Once the beliefs have been identified, ask, "Which small group stated that this belief was important? And which group had a question about or disagreed with this belief? Would one member of the first group state the belief and why it is important to a member of his group?" After the explanation is offered, ask the group that had the question: "Is there anything that was said that would keep you from moving forward with this belief activity?"

The power of this step is that once the tension is acknowledged, it begins to ebb. Thus, learning may occur in a safe and effective way to address individual perspectives within a large group. Moreover, this additional step to clarify and discuss may prepare the group for a subsequent resolution, showing them a creative process to reduce the error or differences between what we want (reference perception) and what we have (perceptual input).

## Alternative Process

After each small group reviews the beliefs list created in step #5, ask each group to write a one-sentence belief statement to reflect what the small group sees is important from the beliefs list. Give them a four-minute deadline, and ask each group to select someone from their group to write the belief statement on a new piece of paper. (If time or paper are in short supply, each group can write its statement on the same page but with a different colored marker.)

You can play music to help energize the group. You will also need to keep track of the time. To emphasize process over final product, urge participants to *synthesize* rather than analyze.

This step is simple and fast. One member from each group comes up front. Tell participants that a break is just around the corner, so hang in there. Ask the group of volunteers to close their eyes and spin around. Or say some "magic" words about forming a unified belief statement. In other words, try to activate their total brain. Then say, "When you open your eyes, don't analyze. Look at the belief statements. Look for one word per person that strikes your heart not your head. Put a dot by that word or underline it." Shoot for identifying four words.

The last step can be taken after a break. Ask for two or three volunteers from this last group to form the "Dream Team." This group's job is to put the four words into a phrase or sentence. They can add color, symbols, music, dance, or anything else to make it come alive for them. We want the dream to become real — a living staff belief statement.

Two examples of belief statements created through this process are: "If it's meant to be, it's up to me!" and "Let's Care, Share, and Preeeeeeee-Pare!"

## Use It or Lose It

Use the belief statement with each other, and if possible practice at home for a period of time to see how it works. This is the practice and experiment stage. It helps to keep an open mind.

**Ask people to make a commitment.**

*Ask for the people promise.* Promise yourself that you will use this belief statement for a period of time. Commit yourself to making it work instead of finding reasons why it won't work. Those involved will also commit to one another. "We will continue to use the staff belief statement." During this time, ask people to outline how they will use the belief statement daily.

It is also important to commit to *contribute* instead of sabotaging the process. Sabotage comes in many forms. It really depends upon one's heart, not one's head. "Can everyone who will give this a chance raise their hands? And if any of you feel for whatever reason that you cannot go forward, can you promise not to stand in the way of those that want to move forward?" If there are people who feel resistant, ask them if they'd be willing to meet later to discuss their issues.

## Keep It Close to Your Heart

When working with students' belief statements and establishing classroom beliefs, emphasize the value of talking about beliefs in non-disciplinary situations. Otherwise "beliefs" simply replace "rules." For example, the question "What do we believe in our class?" gets interpreted by students as a kinder, gentler version of "What are our rules?"

Beliefs are different. Beliefs reflect higher level perceptions of ourselves. Rules are at the program level and only describe desired behaviors. Rules are necessary, but rarely invite the "inside-out" approach to life that is at the heart of *A Connected School*. If students do not have reference perceptions (for example, reference perceptions for what "success" looks like) then they will not reorganize their thinking to bring about the desired changes.

## Use It Daily

**first:** "Daily Successes" is a simple way to begin to align beliefs with behaviors. Each evening before going to bed write two words, phrases, or sentences about ways your thoughts, feelings, actions, or words aligned with your belief statement that day. These notes can become a living record of your efforts to align your behavior with your beliefs.

**second:** Use the belief statement on staff memos and internal building communications. Memos from the administration to staff members can highlight the staff's belief statement. Occasionally share stories of "how we

**At the end of each day, take note of your successes.**

live it" with other staff members.

One staff threw a party to celebrate its belief statement. Staff members gathered after

school to share food, listen to music, and perform skits. Spouses were invited, too. Everyone had so much fun that this Beliefs Party turned into a monthly "SCP"group. (SCP stands for Share, Care, and Party. Initially it was a "Share, Care, and Preeee-Pare" staff belief statement. But it has become Party Central!)

**third:** Hang posters of the belief statement in the staff lounge. Let people fill blank paper with stories about using the belief statement to be the kind of people they want to be. For example, on a billboard declare: "It's September, and this is how we live it." It is important to stick with this practice. Near the end of the year, if the staff has stayed the course, you will notice a difference in what people write. Their comments will be more personal, more descriptive, and more in depth. People love to tell their stories. And when we are living our beliefs, we want to share our stories and learn how others are doing the same. It is a very encouraging process!

Success stories can be summarized and put into print for distribution in mailboxes or at monthly staff meetings. This sharing becomes the fabric of how staff members interact and see themselves. By connecting to colleagues in this way, when there is conflict, we don't see the opposing party as one-dimensional.

**fourth:** Include "Success Circles" in some of your staff meetings. Sit in a circle with a talking stick or some item that represents the school, the staff, or the staff beliefs. Offer each person an opportunity to share a success story of how he or she has acted upon the beliefs statement. Do not force people to share if they are uncomfortable.

This can be a valuable learning opportunity for staff members. Often we don't know what our colleagues think and do beyond limited lunch conversations. Use this time to "take a look at yourself" as a group and — most importantly — **CONNECT!**

# get the picture

Throughout this book we've sprinkled examples of how people have integrated **A Connected School** concepts into their school activities and into their lives. To help keep you focused, here are some more of their stories.

# Keep Asking

**O**ne of the students I work with has a rare genetic disorder that has led to significant physical disabilities. Edwin has some difficulty communicating and his speech is sometimes unintelligible. On his first day at middle school I wanted to make a point of checking in with Edwin to see how he was doing.

I found him in social studies class, and asked him to come out and visit with me in the hall. He told me that school was "terrible." I asked for more specifics and he told me that lunch was bad. I inquired further, and he said it was different than last year. As last year he had been in elementary school, this was certainly true. So I asked him how it was different. He told me there were more choices. Assuming that having too many choices was the problem, I commented in that regard. He said that he did-n't have a problem with the choices, but the student in line in front of him did. We talked about the fact that there was nothing Edwin could do to make another person choose faster.

When I learned that I had pulled Edwin out of social studies class, I said that I shouldn't keep him any longer as I thought I recalled that social studies was his favorite subject. He said no, science was his favorite, but he had missed it today because of lunch.

All of a sudden, the problem became much clearer to me. He was upset about the lunch routine because it caused him to miss science class. Given his physical disabilities, I had been scheming about what we needed to do to make the lunch routine go more smoothly, but that wasn't really the issue. After a lot more probing, Edwin was able to describe his "picture": he wanted to have time to eat lunch *and* get to science on time.

I delved further to help him develop a clear picture of how he "wanted it to be." As an occupational therapist, I am not at Edwin's school every day, so the next step was to get someone at the school to help Edwin implement his plan. I had written down his plan as I talked to him, and he asked to read that to the person who would assist him. Together, he and his assistant developed a plan for the next day, and Edwin went back to class.

Prior to learning about Perceptual Control Theory, I would have given up on Edwin and hoped that someone else could help him. This time, I felt I had the skills to help him figure out what the problem was and work through it.

CARRIE CARLSON
AREA EDUCATION AGENCY #267, IOWA

# Use It Every Day

**O**ne Friday afternoon at the end of the school year, I was caught in the workroom by one of my co-workers who looked and sounded very stressed out. (It has been my experience that many teachers appear this way at the end of the year!) I listened to her for about ten minutes as she talked about her long list of things that were due, things not getting done, and how her students were acting up. After she ran out of steam, I said, "It sounds like you are feeling out of control right now. Do you want to be in control during this difficult time of the year?" She immediately said that she did, and I could see her energize as she contemplated my question. I then asked, "What would it look like if you were in control right now?" She was able to describe her picture of what it would look like and came up with some good suggestions for successfully handling the end-of-the-year commitments that were stressing her out.

One of the things that I like most about these ideas is that they can be used in the course of normal conversation and still be very effective. As a counselor, I have used these ideas many times and have never had someone stop and say, "Are you counseling me right now?" In this particular case, I asked my colleague the questions quite naturally and yet it saved me about twenty minutes in the workroom because I was able to validate her feelings and get her thinking about a solution in a very short amount of time.

JUDY IVORY
CUMBERLAND COUNTY
(NORTH CAROLINA) SCHOOLS

# The Pencil Problem

**S**ince the beginning of school, I have tried to implement ideas that I have learned from Perceptual Control Theory. For example, on the first day of school a student presented me with a common problem — he had forgotten his pencil.

I asked the student how he could solve his problem, and he looked at me as if I was crazy. I told him that I'd let him think about his problem for a few minutes and then check back with him. When I went back to him, repeatedly, his reply was always the same: "I don't have a pencil," as if he wasn't quite sure that I understood the situation. Finally, after letting him stew for about ten minutes, he informed me that his neighbor would let him borrow a pencil.

I have continued in this way throughout the year, asking students how they could solve their own problems themselves. The pencil-less student that I worked with on the first day of school has watched me closely as other students have approached me with the same problem.

One day while we were working on a writing activity, another student raised her hand and told me that she needed a pencil. My reply, of course, was to ask how she could solve that problem. "What is something that you could do to solve your problem of not having a pencil?" While she was trying to figure it out, other students around the room were frantically waving pencils at her. (My class does enjoy sharing and helping others.) However, I wanted her to solve the problem herself, so I informed the class of this. She then said, "I have asked everyone in my team, but no one has a pencil for me." I said, "OK, what else could you do?" She decided that she should ask someone else in the class, and I told her to go ahead. In a matter of moments, her problem was solved, and we were ready to move on.

From out of nowhere, a voice said, "Wow, you are good!" These words came from the young man that had no pencil on the first day of school. We had a brief class discussion on what had happened and what I hoped to accomplish this year in terms of responsibility.

Most of the students have really seemed to grasp this part of PCT and rarely ask me to help them with simple problems, unless they are really stuck. Though the problems are usually minor, my hope is that my students will be able to transfer these problem-solving skills to solve larger problems as well.

JOCEE MCLAURIN
CUMBERLAND COUNTY
(NORTH CAROLINA) SCHOOLS

# Listen Up!

Lamont was an eleven-year-old in the fourth grade. Large for his age, Lamont looked, acted, and dressed like a fifteen- or sixteen-year-old boy. Lamont was often hostile toward adults and did not connect easily to anyone in the school. He was intelligent, yet often chose to not do his work. He was quick to try to aggravate other students.

As building principal, I saw Lamont on many occasions. A sampling of one of our first meetings appears below.

Lamont was asked to leave the room by his teacher after referring to another student as a "faggot." Lamont denied saying it and claimed he did not know the meaning of the word. He refused to look at me and was angry.

I asked him this simple question: "Lamont, have you ever had a good relationship with an adult at school?" He nodded yes. "What was that like?" I asked.

Lamont began to describe his relationship with an adult at his last school. He used limited phrases, but was able to create a picture. Among the important points he made was this: "She respected me."

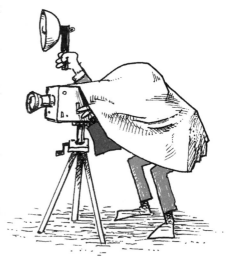

I then asked, "How did you know she respected you? What did she do or say?" Lamont was able to describe what his picture of the teacher's respect looked like, using phrases such as "she listened." I continued to probe: "How did you know she was listening?" Lamont was able to identify specific behaviors that led him to feel safe and connected to this individual.

After questioning and listening, I summarized what Lamont had told me: "You felt close to the adult because she listened to you, by sitting closely and looking into your eyes. Sometimes, she even touched your hand. You felt this person was honest with you, and while you didn't always like what she said, you always knew she was up front. Is that right?" Lamont nodded. He had moved himself in his chair and was not looking at me.

I continued, "Lamont, that is the kind of relationship that I want to have with you — one where you feel listened to and where you feel you can trust me. Do you want that same relationship?" Lamont's eyes began to fill with tears. I then told him that I thought relationships like that took time and asked him if he would like to spend some time with me. We made a plan that I would stop by his classroom several times a week and check in with him. He then looked at me and acted politely for the remainder of the conversation.

I met with Lamont on many subsequent occasions. While our work together did not result in a miraculous change in his behavior, he began making baby steps. I believe that helping him understand Perceptual Control Theory helped him make connections to others. At the same time, he began to understand that there were logical consequences to misbehavior and this understanding helped him feel a sense of security. Questioning him revealed to both me and him that he had felt manipulated into behaving in the past. Self-evaluation also helped him think things through and allowed him to have a sense of power over his own behavior. We continually worked to bump things up — thinking about who he wanted to be, what we believe as a school, etc.

Lamont is truly in the process of reinventing himself. He grew to believe that I would listen to him, yet would hold him and everyone else accountable for their actions. I will always remember the high I felt when my birthday rolled around, and there on my desk was a dollar-store card (bought by a kid who didn't have a dollar) with a warm, handwritten note and picture tucked inside.

**JACQUELINE RAPP**
JOHNSON CITY (NEW YORK)
CENTRAL SCHOOL DISTRICT

# The Big Picture

**M**y fourth-hour class is a cooperative class that I share with another teacher, Elizabeth Hall. Half of the students in this class have some sort of learning difficulty. During this last quarter, students have been reading *To Kill a Mockingbird*. Some of them choose to work in groups, while others read by themselves. We gather together regularly as a class to discuss the novel.

Elizabeth and I have noticed that some of the students wear headphones, listening to music while doing their work. The music is not loud, and they are completing their work. I understand this: as a graduate student, I often listened to music while studying.

The appearance of headphones has got us thinking about what our duties as teachers are. Part of our job is showing the kids how to act

responsibly. How better to do this than by allowing them to use things they enjoy responsibly. I was surprised at the number of students who used the headphones appropriately without disturbing others. We allowed them to fulfill their desire to be autonomous while operating in the confines of our classroom — as long as they did so responsibly. Isn't that what our ultimate goal is as educators — to teach kids how to be productive in society while not abandoning their individuality? I believe that I have a stronger relationship with my fourth-hour students because of my ability to stick to the bigger picture of education.

JEANNETTE ROBBINS
CUMBERLAND COUNTY
(NORTH CAROLINA) SCHOOLS

# bibliography

Boffey, Barnes. *Reinventing Yourself.* Chapel Hill, NC: New View Publications, 1993.

Brandes, Beth Harris, and Judy B. Ingold. *Get Real: A Practical Guide to Leading Adolescent Groups.* Milwaukee, WI: Families International, Inc., 1997.

Brooks, Jacqueline Grannon, and Martin Brooks. *In Search of Understanding: The Case for Constructivist Classrooms.* Alexandria, Virginia: Association for Supervision and Curriculum Development, 1993.

Caine, Geoffrey; Renate Nummela Caine; and Sam Crowell. *Mindshifts.* Tucson, AZ: Zephyr Press, 1994

Capra, Frijof. *The Web of Life.* New York: Anchor Books Doubleday, 1996

Canfield, Jack, and Harold C. Wells. *100 Ways to Enhance Self-Concept in the Classroom.* Englewood Cliffs, NJ: Prentice Hall, 1976.

*Class Meetings.* Educators Training Center, 117 East 8th Street, Suite 810, Long Beach, CA 90813.

Covey, Stephen R. *The Seven Habits of Highly Effective People.* New York: Simon and Schuster, 1989.

Csikszentmihalyi, Mihaly. *Flow: The Psychology of Optimal Experience.* New York: HarperCollins, 1991.

DePorter, Bobbi; Mark Reardon; and Sarah Singer-Nourie. *Quantum Teaching.* Needham Heights, MA: Allyn & Bacon, 1999.

Dreikurs, Rudolph, and Vicki Soltz. *Children: The Challenge.* New York: Duell, Sloan and Pearce, 1964.

Dunn, Steven E., and R. Bruce Williams, *Brain Compatible Learning for the Block Schedule.* Arlington Heights, IL: SkyLight, 2000.

Fluegelman, Andrew (editor). *The New Games Book.* Garden City, NY: Dolphin Books/Doubleday, 1976.

Gibbs, Jeanne. *Tribes.* Santa Rosa, CA: CenterSource Publications, 1990.

Glasser, Naomi. *What Are You Doing?* New York: HarperCollins 1980.

Glasser, William. *Control Theory.* New York: HarperCollins, 1984.

_____. *Control Theory in the Classroom.* New York: HarperCollins 1987.

_____. *The Quality School, 2nd Edition.* New York: HarperCollins, 1992.

Glazer, Steven (editor). *The Heart of Learning: Spirituality in Education.* New York: Penguin Putman, 1999.

Gonder, Peggy Odell, and Donald Hymes. *Improving School Climate & Culture: AASA Critical Issues Report.* Arlington, VA: American Association of School Administrators, 1994.

Good, E. Perry. *In Pursuit of Happiness.* Chapel Hill, NC: New View Publications, 1987.

_____. *It's Finally OK to Be the Boss.* Chapel Hill, NC: New View Publications, 1999.

_____. *Happy Hour Guide.* Chapel Hill, NC: New View Publications, 1989.

_____. *Helping Kids Help Themselves.* Chapel Hill, NC: New View Publications, 1992.

_____. *Overall Direction.* Chapel Hill, NC: New View Publications, 1996.

Gossen, Diane Chelsom. *Control Theory in Action.* Saskatoon, SASK: Chelsom Consultants, 1989.

_____. *My Child Is a Pleasure to Live With.* Saskatoon, SASK: Chelsom Consultants, 1989.

_____. *Restitution: Restructuring School Discipline*, 2nd Edition. Chapel Hill, NC: New View Publications, 1996.

_____. *Restitution Facilitator's Guide*, 2nd Edition. Chapel Hill, NC: New View Publications, 1998.

_____ and Judy Anderson. *Creating the Conditions: Leadership for Quality Schools.* Chapel Hill, NC: New View Publications, 1996.

Hallowell, Edward M. *Connect: 12 Vital Ties That Open Your Heart, Lengthen Your Life, and Deepen Your Soul.* New York: Pocket Books, 1999.

Jensen, Eric. *Completing the Puzzle: The Brain-Based Approach.* Del Mar, CA: Turning Point Publishing, 1996.

Karns, Michelle. *How to Create Positive Relationships with Students: A Handbook of Group Activities and Teaching Strategies.* Champaign, IL: Research Press, 1994.

Kerman, Sam; Tom Kimball; and Mary Martin. *Teacher Expectation, Student Achievement.* Bloomington, IN: Phi Delta Kappa, 1980.

Kohn, Alfie. *Beyond Discipline: From Compliance to Community.* Alexandria, VA: Association for Supervision and Curriculum Development, 1996.

_____. *The Brighter Side of Human Nature.* Boulder, CO: Basic Books, 1990.

_____. *No Contest: The Case Against Competition.* Boston: Houghton Mifflin, 1992.

_____. *Punished by Rewards.* Boston: Houghton Mifflin, 1993.

Kriete, Roxann. *The Morning Meeting Book.* Greenfield, MA: Northeast Foundation For Children,1999

Lebow, Rob, and Randy Spitzer. *Accountability: Freedom and Responsibility Without Control.* San Francisco: Berrett-Koehlerm, 2002.

Marzano, Robert; Debra J. Pickering; Daisy E. Arrecondo; Guy J. Blackburn; Ronald S. Brandt; and Cerylle A. Moffett. *Dimensions of Learning.* Alexandria, VA: Association for Supervision and Curriculum Development, 1992.

McTighe, Jay, and Grant Wiggins. *Understanding by Design.* Alexandria, VA: Association for Supervision and Curriculum Development, 1998.

Moos, R.H. *Evaluating Educational Environments: Procedures, Measures, Findings, and Policy Implications.* San Francisco: Jossey-Bass, 1979.

Peacock, Fletcher. *Water the Flowers.* Montreal, Quebec: Open Heart Publishing, 2001.

Peck, M Scott. *The Road Less Traveled.* New York: Simon & Schuster, 1979.

Powers, William T. *Behavior: The Control of Perception.* Chicago: Aldine, 1973.

_____. *Making Sense of Behavior.* New Canaan, CT: Benchmark Publications, 1998.

Rohnke, Karl. *Silver Bullets: A Guide To Initiative Problems, Adventure Games, And Trust Activities.* Dubuque, IA: Kendall/Hunt Publishing, 1984.

Ronis, Diane. *Brain Compatible Assessments.* Arlington Heights, IL: SkyLight, 2000.

Rosenberg, Marshall. *Nonviolent Communications.* Encinitas, CA: PuddleDancer Press, 1999.

Ross, Rupert. *Returning to the Teachings: Exploring Aboriginal Justice.* Toronto, Canada: Penguin Books, 1996

Schrumpf, Fred; Sharon Freiburg; and David Skadden. *Life Lessons for Young Adolescents: An Advisory Guide for Teachers.* Champaign, IL: Research Press, 1993.

Simon, Sidney B.; Leland W. Howe; and Howard Kirschenbaum. *Values Clarification: A Handbook of Practical Strategies for Teachers and Students.* New York: Hart Publishing, 1972.

Smith, Glenn, and Kathy Tomberlin. *Quality Time for Quality Kids.* Chapel Hill, NC: New View Publications, 1992.

Switzer, Delores. *Teacher's Guide to In Pursuit of Happiness.* Chapel Hill, NC: New View Publications, 1992.

Sullo, Robert A. *Teach Them to Be Happy.* Chapel Hill, NC: New View Publications, 1989.

Sylwester. Robert. *A Celebration of Neurons: An Educator's Guide to the Human Brain*, Alexandria, VA: Association for Supervision and Curriculum Development, 1995.

Wheatley, Margaret J., *Leadership & the New Science: Discovering Order in a Chaotic World*. San Francisco: Berrett-Koehler, 1999.

Williams, R. Bruce, and Steven E. Dunn. *Brain Compatible Learning for the Block*. Arlington Heights, IL: Skylight, 2000

Wubbolding, Robert E. *Using Reality Therapy*. New York: HarperCollins, 1988.

# about the authors

**E. Perry Good** is a popular speaker, trainer, and counselor. A senior faculty member of the International Association for Applied Control Theory, she has conducted more than 3,000 workshops in the United States and throughout the world — Australia, Canada, Croatia, Indonesia, Norway, and Slovenia. Her audiences have included educators and counselors; mental health and social services personnel; youth services providers; drug-abuse prevention specialists; and corporate executives.

A native of North Carolina, Perry also has lived in France, San Francisco (where she worked on *Sesame Street*), and New York City (teaching and counseling on the Lower East Side). She now lives in Chapel Hill with her husband, Fred. Their daughter, Jessica, is a social worker in New York City. Perry is the author of *In Pursuit of Happiness*, *Helping Kids Help Themselves*, *Overall Direction*, and *It's Finally OK to Be the Boss*.

**Jeff Grumley** is a principal of the Grumley Group PC, an educational consulting and counseling business. He teaches students, parents, teachers, and people interested in PCT as a senior instructor in IAACT.

For the past twenty years he has taught in diverse settings from public education to teen recovery centers.
He frequently travels in northern Canada (the
Northwest Territories and Nunavit) and Iceland. Jeff
has a doctorate in counseling and is ordained as a
United Methodist minister. Jeff regularly participates
in Lakota (Native American) ceremonies. He loves
reading and reciting poetry. He lives with his wife,
Therese, and teenage daughters in Rockford, Illinois.

**Shelley Roy** is president of Synergy Transition
Consulting. A recognized leader in human resource
development, Shelley has worked with thousands of
adults in a wide range of learning situations. For more
than ten years, she has provided ongoing facilitation
to more than seventy improvement teams. Shelley has
consulted throughout the country and abroad on leadership, human behavior, effective communication,
models of teaching, interagency collaboration, effective schools research, and other areas related to
change and building productive teams. She has taught
in the K-12 system and at the university level in West
Berlin, Germany; the Navajo Reservation, New
Mexico; Junction City, Kansas; and Leigh, Nebraska.
She lives in Sartell, Minnesota.

# Make your school A Connected School.

For information about how to bring the concepts described in this book to your system or school call us at New View. **Perry Good**, **Jeff Grumley**, and **Shelley Roy** will design workshops around your specific needs such as a one-day overview or a four-day seminar that focuses on personal and systems change. Another option is to send a leadership team to one of our regularly scheduled seminars, which are held each June in Chapel Hill, N.C., or January in Hilton Head, S.C. For a brochure and information about these upcoming events, call **New View at (800) 441-3604**.

*"Perceptual Control Theory provides you with a process to define the kind of school district, school, class, and community that you want yours to be. It forms the basis of effectively working on culture, the life blood of any organization."*

**Larry Rowe**, *Superintendent*
*Johnson City (N.Y.) Community School District*

**BY THE CASE** Get your whole staff involved in *A Connected School* by ordering them by the case. There are 30 books per case at a 30% discount — making the discount price $315.00, a savings of $135.00. Or you may order individual books at $15.00 per copy. Purchase orders can be sent to:

**NEW VIEW * P.O. Box 3021 * Chapel Hill, NC 27515-3021**
**Phone (800) 441-3604 * Fax (919) 942-3760**
**www.newviewpublications.com**